GENEALOGICAL RESEARCH
on the WEB

Diane K. Kovacs

NEAL-SCHUMAN NETGUIDE SERIES

Neal-Schuman Publishers, Inc.
New York   London

Published by Neal-Schuman Publishers, Inc.
100 Varick Street
New York, NY 10013

Printed and bound in the United States of America.

ISBN: 1–55570–430–1

Contents

TAKE ADVANTAGE OF THE WEB SITE AND E-MAIL THE AUTHOR!

The Web-based activities use hands-on guided learning to enable you to obtain the knowledge you need to effectively use genealogical resources on the Internet or to assist others in doing so. The Web forms in each activity allow you to report your experiences, discuss your conclusions, and ask the author questions as you do each activity. You may also e-mail the author/ instructor with questions or for assistance as you use *Genealogical Research on the Web* or the Web-based materials.

Remember registering and using the interactive hands-on activities of each unit is free and simple. Just follow these three steps:

1. Access the Companion Web site by connecting to www.kovacs.com/ genbook/genbook.html.
2. Complete the Web-based registration form and submit it.
3. The author/instructor will contact you through e-mail and explain how to get started.

List of Figures

4. How to Locate International, African American, and Native American Ancestors; Heraldry and Lineage Societies

Foreword

They say, "Two's company, three's a crowd." Not always. People like me once thought that the computer was the perfect company for genealogy. Little did we know that just around the corner of time was a third most important companion: the Internet.

Time was when genealogy was a rather lonely business. There were occasional trips to the library, but no library gave access to all the information that could be available. There might be some trips to genealogical conferences, for those who could afford them. There would be occasional opportunities for family get-togethers, although not all family members might share one's interest in charting the family's history. And of course there were those letters to other genealogists, hopeful but not invariably productive.

For the most part the genealogist gathered information slowly by whatever means were possible, sat at home entering the pertinent data on charts, and bemoaned the fact that so much more was needed but seemingly unattainable. In this the genealogist normally worked alone. Some were more productive than others. Some had more contact with other genealogists. Some every now and then hit upon highly productive veins of golden information. Yet even among the most experienced genealogists there was the feeling of being alone in addressing the specific task.

The Internet has changed that picture. The Internet has made possible the widest imaginable availability of genealogical information pertinent to one's needs. In genealogy the Internet has become the Great Equalizer.

Yet there is a trade-off. Information from the Internet is not available at a price of simply saying "Open, Sesame!" One has to learn how to use the Internet with specific attention being paid to where to find desired genealogical information. In this there is an embarrassment of riches, which means that for some it could be a situation analogous to sailing across the ocean without knowing how to use a compass.

As so often is the case, many people facing this problem think first of going to the library and learning from that respected, trusty guardian of information, the librarian. The problem here is that the Internet is new to all of us, even librarians. As an old genealogical saying once had it, "Our families might not all have come to America in the first boat, but we're all in the same boat now."

Diane K. Kovacs has geared her book *Genealogical Research on the Web* to the needs of librarians. As an academic librarian and private genealogist herself, she has faced the problems personally and put in much effort to study and find solutions. It is a problem that grows every day as new Web sites provide additional opportunities for more people to present information of interest to genealogists.

Death records, for example, with much helpful information for genealogists, can be found by the millions in the Social Security Administration's Death Master File. However, the U.S. Social Security program began in 1935, and we can safely say that the name of no person born prior to the 19th century will appear in those records. Where else might one look? As Diane Kovacs's book demonstrates, there are numerous Web sites giving information from or about cemetery sites, war records, pension records, church records, wills, and other records, not to mention the millions of individually compiled family histories.

Birth records, marriage records, individual genealogies, family histories, immigration records, Native American tribal records, African American records, Mexican Border Crossing Records, ship manifests, heraldry and coat of arms sources, adoption records—there are literally thousands and thousand of Web sites with information of value to the genealogist, and Diane's book shows how and where to find them; in many cases she tells what and where they are, and who they will help.

This book names and describes the 10 Best Sites for genealogists and then goes on to list numerous other sites. It emphasizes references, documentation, and communications with other genealogists, and additionally features throughout a Web-based workshop to help users learn by doing. It also gives users the opportunity of using the Internet to get in direct touch with the author for problem solving.

The book should be invaluable not only to librarians, but also to the professional genealogist and the avid private researcher. It shows, it teaches, and it expedites. The author does not neglect some of the serious aspects of where genealogy can go wrong, but strives to make the reader aware of the need to evaluate the discovered information and the need to know something about the history of the time and place being researched. Diane Kovacs gives information on where to find more information on these topics, as well as a bibliography of other instructional Web and printed sources.

This is a much needed book. Sources on the Internet have become as vast as the world they treat of, and those sources of general and special interest to the genealogist share that vastness. To find one's way around with effectiveness and reasonable speed, one needs a roadmap. This book is just the right kind of roadmap.

EUGENE STRATTON
Author of *Applied Genealogy*

Acknowledgments

Always my gratitude to my husband, Michael Kovacs and to his family, without whom I don't think I'd ever have started this book. Thank you to my mother, Jean Ann Engelbrecht (Finch), for tolerating my repeated questioning and rehearsal of my genealogical research—my gratitude for the endless e-mail correspondence and also for sharing her files. I would like to offer special thanks to my family. They contributed hours of telephone, postal mail, and just "skin" to this work. In particular, I'd like to thank Grandma Lucille and her little brother Great-Uncle Harold, my father-in-law Joseph Gabor Kovacs, my brother-in-law's little brother Daniel Palos, and many other darling people I have the great fortune to call family relations. Before this book was completed, Grandma Alice Jean Finch (Wilson) left us. Her boxes and boxes of records and newspaper clippings made my research fascinating and productive. I miss her very much.

The Illinois and Ohio centrism of many examples in this book is because those are the states where both my birth and marriage families have resided for the past century or more. The Illinois State Archives and the Ohio Historical Society, as well as the respective state libraries have provided many valuable tools for the genealogical researchers exploring those states' records to use on the Internet.

Thank you very much to Charles Harmon—who has more patience than any man I know—my editor Michael Kelley, and all the staff of Neal-Schuman for their competent and thorough work in bringing this book to fruition.

Preface

Each year thousands of people work with librarians, archivists, genealogists, and researchers as they research their family history or compile genealogies. In the last decade, the Internet has become an increasingly important tool for all these genealogists, professional and amateur. The Web helps to access indexes and sources of genealogical information, as well as facilitate communication and establish inter-personal networking. The Internet has transformed the research capabilities for the serious professional, amateur, or recreational genealogical researcher. *Genealogical Research on the Web* and the companion Web-based workshop is designed to be an informative, innovative, and exciting departure point for anyone interested in embarking on this journey of discovery.

The Internet enhances genealogical research in three key areas:

1. Reference: The Internet provides access to indexes and compilation notes of primary, secondary, and tertiary genealogical information.
2. Documentation: The Internet provides access to scanned images or actual full text of primary (e.g., vital records, historical census, immigration and military records, newspaper, and other contemporary accounts in letters, diaries, deeds, wills etc.), and secondary and tertiary genealogical sources (e.g., genealogical journals and magazines, published family histories, etc.).
3. Communications and Travel: The Internet assists identifying and communicating with genealogical researchers and subjects, including one's own family; seeking education and training opportunities, engaging in correspondence (including ordering information for document copies and research services), and planning travel to libraries, archives, and other locations holding genealogical documentation, as well as shared data.

Genealogical Research on the Web has its own story of origin. In 1996 I began teaching workshops on genealogical research on the Internet. By that time, I had already enjoyed many years of experience with genealogical research as a librarian at Kent State University. I worked with patrons doing their own research while also researching my own family. The potential of Internet-accessible genealogical information was becoming very attractive. I first taught "Genealogical Research on the Internet" in 1996 for the Ohio Valley Area Libraries (OVAL). I opened my remarks at that first genealogical research on the Internet workshop—and at every workshop I've taught since then—with a frank confession. As an academic reference librarian, I had sometimes dreaded working with genealogical researchers. My dread was not of the patron, but a result of the inadequacy of our local collection for working with the many genealogical researchers who visited our library. All too frequently, I had to say "No, I can't help you," or "No, we don't have ____." Fill in the blank: full-text census records, immigration rolls, military records, family history texts, diaries, etc.

I'm pleased to report that the resources currently made available to librarians through the Internet make it much more efficient and pleasant for both librarians and genealogical researchers to work together. Although librarians may still frequently have to admit, "No, we don't have that," now by using the Internet, they can say, "I think I can help you figure out what library or organization has that publication, or archival material." And librarians may be able to tell the researcher what organizations are providing indexes to records, ordering information and forms, or even making those records available full-text online.

Suitable for any researcher, *Genealogical Research on the Web* will be useful to everyone with an interest in seeking genealogical information. In addition, it was also constructed to be an invaluable aid to librarians in creating genealogical programs and training. It will be of equal interest to every professional—public librarians, academic librarians, and archivists—that helps others in their genealogical pursuits. Librarians should feel free to choose to share the contents of this workshop-in-a-book with patrons who are researching genealogy. They may wish to conduct locally-based workshops employing the book and Web-based training materials or loan the book directly to patrons for their own self-study. The activities are standard HTML-based Web pages and may be downloaded, adapted, and used for local staff and patron training as long as the copyright statements remain intact.

All researchers interacting with these Web-based learning activities will gain practical knowledge. This interactive research experience—including direct contact via e-mail with me, the author—goes way beyond "just reading" about genealogical reference resources on the Internet. In order to discover and utilize some of the most exciting research tools currently available on the Internet, these explorations are presented in an easy, step-by-step way. *Genealogical Research on the Web* and its companion Web-based activities only require that readers have and know how to use basic Internet access, e-mail software, and a recent version of Web browser. No prior genealogical research experience is necessary.

The four parts of *Genealogical Research on the Web* follow the same format. Each covers a different, vital aspect of genealogical research in the context of the Internet. This essential background information is illustrated by personal genealogical research success stories shared from other researchers. Each part also contains learning activities designed to give you guided practice doing genealogical research on the Internet. These can be found on the Web, as well as included in this book. The Web-based activities, teaching hands-on guided skills, enable researchers to obtain both the knowledge and practice needed to effectively use genealogical resources on the Internet.

Access the Web-based activities by connecting to www.kovacs.com/ns/ genbook/genbook.html. Type the requested registration information into the Web form and click on the "submit" button. You will receive a login and password through e-mail, within a day or so, that tells you how to get started. Access to the Web-based activities and other materials also gives you access to myself, the author, as an instructor. I will work through e-mail with anyone working on the interactive learning activities or responding to the discussion questions in the Web-based text. Web forms in each activity allow you to report your experiences, discuss your conclusions, and ask me questions as you do each activity. You may also e-mail me with questions or for assistance as you use the book or Web-based materials. I will provide feedback and support if you request it through e-mail or the Web-based activity forms. You will always have someone to ask questions of and share your experiences with as you work. Periodically, group online discussions will be scheduled for each part and individuals who have purchased this book and registered for the Web-based workshop will be invited to attend—all at no additional cost. Individuals can share their experiences in learning about and doing genealogical research on the Internet with each other.

The Web site also hosts a compilation of the core genealogical reference sites discussed in *Genealogical Research on the Web* and will be updated frequently as new sites become available. The genealogical reference sites discussed form a core reference collection for practical genealogical reference services. The accessibility of this information and the increasing quantity of high-quality genealogical information on the Internet make this a very engaging genealogical reference resource.

Organization

Part 1, "How to Get Started: The Basics of Genealogical Research on the Internet," explores fundamentals by addressing important preliminary questions. What is genealogical research? What is family history research? Perhaps most importantly: Why do genealogical or family history research? The basics of genealogical research in the context of the Internet are discussed, including the minimum Internet access and software required, and an overview of the types of information available on or through the Internet. Reference interviews with genealogical researchers can be a challenge. We'll explore ideas for successful outcomes. A major component of Part 1 is the evaluation of genealogical information found on the Internet. It is essential to always consider "the source" of any information in any format, but on the Internet it can be a more proximate concern. There is no overall quality control for genealogical research materials on the Internet. Some sites will be well-documented and accurately compiled and others will be little more than family fantasies. Some full-text collections will be scanned records, images, and professionally verified indexes. Other sites will just be junk that someone made up. As long as we keep the problems in mind, the benefits of using the Internet as a tool for genealogical research are great.

In Part 2, "How to Find and Use Basic Genealogical Reference and Documentation Tools on the Web" discusses the ten "best" genealogical reference tools on the Internet. It explores government resources from the Social Security Death Records and the National Archives and Records Administration to popular Web sites like Ancestry.com and Cyndi's Genealogical Homepage. The activities for Part 2 will give you hands-on experience using these reference tools for your genealogical research.

Part 3, "How to Network with Living Family Members and/or Fellow Genealogical Researchers," focuses on the challenges and rewards of communicating and networking with fellow genealogical researchers. This part will look at how to find fellow researchers and family members, individually and through discussion lists and newsgroups, as well as how to collaborate through e-mail effectively. And it will briefly address how family data is shared on the Internet. This part also confronts a practical reality of genealogical research: quality genealogical research requires documentation. It is not enough to use family anecdotes or coincidental name similarities, or even previously published family history books as support for quality genealogy. Researchers need to be able to locate and obtain copies of documentation where possible. Many types of documentation can be ordered from library, archival, or organizational sources through postal or electronic correspondence. However, genealogical researchers will frequently need to travel. Sometimes this means driving to the local courthouse and other times it may mean flying back to the "old country." Part 3 will point to Internet resources that will help you plan your genealogical research travel and correspondence effectively.

Genealogical research for most citizens of the United States is a multi-cultural, multi-lingual and often political process. Our family histories are intertwined with our national history and international origins. Part 4, "How to Locate International, African American, and Native American Ancestors; Heraldry and Lineage Societies," looks at some special areas of genealogical research in which resources on the Internet can be very helpful. Specifically this part pays special attention to international (multi-country), Native American, and African American genealogical resources. This part also investigates heraldry and lineage societies in addition to other related genealogical issues.

Genealogical Research on the Web concludes with "Sources," which includes three information collections. "The Internet Genealogy Ready-Reference E-Library," is a selected annotated webliography of the best genealogical reference tools on the Internet. The companion Web site version of this collection—where each of these individual sites will be hyperlinked and available with a click of your mouse—will be updated frequently and consistently.

Because no one workshop or book can cover all facets of genealogical research, "More Readings About Genealogical Research on the Internet" includes an annotated bibliography of further readings in genealogical research on and off the Internet.

Finally, a concise and useful glossary of genealogy and Internet terms is provided.

Genealogical Research on the Web is an invitation to join a world of explorers; each beginning their journey from a modest but vital place. All researchers delve into the discovery of their own life story as the culmination and continuation of the human drama we call family. We learn our own stories by helping one another with research. Because of the interactive nature of this book, I hope to hear from many of you and help in ways both practical and supportive. Indeed, I learn with every discovery of a workshop participant. In return, I hope this "workshop in a book" and the access to interactive activities helps your important researching succeed.

Part 1
How to Get Started: The Basics of Genealogical Research on the Internet

"Death records?" the wood nymph (librarian) said when I asked her. "They're over at the courthouse. We're going to get all that kind of stuff put on the computer some day, so all you have to do is call it up right here." She pointed vaguely toward a couple of computers that sat unused, on a table. "But right now you're going to have to go over to the courthouse. Up on the tenth floor. Archives Department." (George, 1997:208).

"While I was in the shower, I thought about the obvious advantages of changing a name on a family tree. General Sherman's name on the Johnson lineage chart had kept Camille Atchison out of an organization she felt passionately about belonging to. But if General William Tecumseh Sherman became William Thomas Sherman, a Georgia farmer wounded in service to the Confederacy, could Camille take the revised pedigree chart and say 'Big mistake. Clean slate,' and be admitted? How much proof would she have to come up with?" (George, 1997:205).

This part discusses the basics of genealogical research and what can and cannot be done using the Internet. Issues of documentation and evaluation of sources are addressed as well.

What Is Genealogical or Family History Research?

These terms are often used interchangeably but what do they really mean?

The terms are related but emphasize different types of research. Family history may involve genealogical research and the creation of a "family tree" or "lineage" but it is also a general historical account or investigation of a family's activities and involvement in or reaction to historical events. Family history may also be narrative and documentation of family life in general in a particular geographic location and time.

Genealogical research involves documenting the lines of ancestors and descendants through records of births, marriages, deaths, and other legally defined events. It may or may not include a general historical account. The following definitions help to clarify discussion of genealogical and family history research:

According to *The American Heritage® Dictionary of the English Language*, Third Edition (searched through www.dictionary.com/):

'ge·ne·al·o·gy' is defined as:

1. A record or table of the descent of a person, family, or group from an ancestor or ancestors; a family tree.
2. Direct descent from an ancestor; lineage or pedigree.
3. The study or investigation of ancestry and family histories.

A 'family tree' is:

1. A genealogical diagram of a family's ancestry.
2. The ancestors and descendants of a family considered as a group.

A family is:

1. a. A fundamental social group in society typically consisting of a man and woman and their offspring.
   b. Two or more people who share goals and values, have long-term commitments to one another, and reside usually in the same dwelling place.
2. All the members of a household under one roof.
3. A group of persons sharing common ancestry. See Usage Note at collective noun.
4. Lineage, especially distinguished lineage.

A lineage is:

1. a. Direct descent from a particular ancestor; ancestry.
   b. Derivation.
2. The descendants of a common ancestor considered to be the founder of the line (1996,1992).

Genealogical research is basically the process of discovering one's family. Genealogical research tries to answer an essential question: From whom are we descended? Family history research relies on the results of genealogical research. Once we know whom we are descended from, we can look for where, when, how, and why they lived, moved, or were affected by historical trends and events. This is a two-way process. We also need to know something of where, when, and how our ancestors lived in order to locate documentation of their relationships to us. Eugene Stratton in his classic book *Applied Genealogy* describes how people and history are always interactive in any genealogical search:

"Every human being has a father and a mother. The heart of genealogy is merely determining as correctly as possible who the father and mother of any given person were . . . the genealogist who neglects history has only a list of names that are really ciphers, and genealogy becomes void" (1988:2–3).

Genealogical research frequently requires historical research. In order to find out whom we are descended from, we may need to find out where they came from and when. Historical legal conventions, economic and political changes, language use and changes, and even naming conventions all affect the successful pursuit of genealogical information. The most basic example of the need for historical knowledge and understanding is knowing if there are birth, marriage, and/or death records for a particular time and place and if there were, where are they?; who has them?; how were they recorded? The ancestor you research may have lived in a time and place when records of birth, marriage, and death were maintained by individual families, a central government or religious organization maintained records, or maybe they lived at a time when no records were maintained. All of these factors will affect genealogical research.

The introduction of the Internet to genealogical research has transformed the searching process. For librarians and genealogists looking for United States social history data, there are databases such as the Library of Congress American Memory Project (http://memory.loc.gov/), and the Making of America Project (http://moa.umdl.umich.edu.—University of Michigan and http://library5.library.cornell.edu/moa/—Cornell University). The American Memory Project is a remarkable growing collection of digitized photographs, movies, sound recordings, as well as historical printed materials that relate to the history and cultures of the United States. The Making of America Project is a project of Cornell University and University of Michigan to compile collections of searchable page images for more than 6,600 books and 50,8–0 s/urnal articles scanned from historical books, journals, and other documents. The National Library of Canada is also making a number of digital libraries of historical documents, recordings, and photographs available through their Web site, www.nlc-bnc.ca/. Other national libraries and museums around the world are undertaking similar projects. Use Cyndi's List (www.CyndisList.com/), and search under the category "Libraries, Archives & Museums General Library Sites" to find digitized historical collections for other countries and projects. There will be lots more about Cyndi's List in Parts 2, 3, and 4.

Why Do People Do Genealogical Research?

Each individual has their own unique reasons for beginning genealogical research. Some of the broad reasons include:

- A general desire to know who and where you came from.
- Curiosity about possible famous ancestors or your ancestor's involvement in famous historical events.
- Medical history to assess your or your children's risks of genetic disease, cancer, and other illnesses related to heredity.
- Adopted persons looking for their birth parents, or birth parents looking for the children they gave up for adoption.
- Professional genealogists doing someone else's genealogical research.
- Scholars (historians and others) researching family histories.
- Teachers assigning genealogical research as a technique for teaching history that might be relevant to their students' family history.

Although the reasons people have for beginning genealogical research vary, the basic research process remains quite similar. Some exceptions include family medical history research and adoption searches. The specific information for medical genealogical research may be indirect or unavailable. Adoptive child and parent research is a challenge because of the interpersonal dynamics and potential for emotional disruption.

How Does the Internet Support Genealogical Research?

The Internet "enhances" genealogical research in three important ways:

- Reference: Access to indexes and compilation notes of primary, secondary, and tertiary genealogical information.
- Documentation: Access to scanned images or actual full text of primary (e.g., vital records, historical census, immigration and military records, newspaper, and other contemporary accounts in letters, diaries, deeds, wills, etc.), secondary and tertiary genealogical sources (e.g., genealogical journals and magazines, published family histories, etc.).
- Communications and Travel: Identifying and communicating with genealogical researchers including one's own family; including education and training opportunities, correspondence: (including ordering information for document copies and research.

Some of the types of genealogical and historical data that can be found on the Internet include:

- Indexes and ordering information, as well as some vital records and statistics (birth, death, marriage, census, immigration records, etc.).
- Classified Directories and Collections of Internet Genealogical Resources (Metasites).
- Personal Family History Pages.
- Searchable Databases of Personal Family History Pages.
- Searchable Indexes for Commercially Collected Data Products.
- Searchable Indexes for Government Collected Data Products.
- Genealogical Discussion Groups and Usenet Newsgroups.
- Genealogical Freeware and Shareware.
- Genealogical Organizations: City, County, and State Genealogical or Historical Society Pages.

In Part 2, we'll look at the "best" genealogical reference and some documentation sites for locating these types of information.

Genealogical research requires access to primary data about family histories. There is some debate among genealogical researchers and librarians about how to categorize different levels of information. Some feel that the copies made by scanning or other mechanisms are not primary documents in and of themselves. Because of this there is also some debate on whether the Internet can be said to be able to provide information at the primary source level. It is also a fact that vital records, such as birth and death certificates, may have been created some time after the actual event and may be second-hand accounts of the event. Other records are actually hand-written or typed copies of older records made by clerks in an effort to preserve decaying original primary documents. Generally it is agreed that there are three levels of genealogical data:

- Primary sources.
- Secondary sources.
- Tertiary sources.

Primary sources include documentation by contemporary authorities or witnesses. Examples of primary sources are birth, marriage, census and death records, probate, land, church, military, bible, contemporary letters, gravestone, court, and many other records.

Secondary sources are books, articles, stories, copies etc. based on primary sources. Good secondary sources document the primary sources, including interviews with eyewitnesses that were used in the production. Some genealogical researchers view vital records that have been scanned or transcribed from earlier versions as secondary sources. Internet-published scanned images or transcriptions of primary sources are realistically considered secondary sources. Secondary sources vary greatly in their value. Secondary sources that were written contemporarily with reference to interviews with living people can be very valuable. Secondary sources with good documentation of the primary sources are most desirable. Unfortunately, many secondary sources are written years, even centuries, after the fact. Also, unfortunately, many secondary sources are based on family beliefs, legends, or the writers desire to glorify the family history rather than document facts of family genealogy.

"In genealogy the value of secondary sources can range from being virtually useless to being virtually indisputable, but in any case for them to be accepted by the genealogist as sufficient evidence by themselves to establish genealogical relationships, they must have one indispensable element: they must be documented! Secondary sources must provide an audit trail to show where the ultimate information came from" (Stratton, 1988:52).

Tertiary sources are documents or records based on secondary sources only. These are of limited value unless they have used well-documented secondary sources such as journal articles in scholarly genealogical journals or high quality secondary sources compiled from clearly documented primary sources.

For more in-depth discussion, Eugene Stratton in *Applied Genealogy* (1988) defines primary and secondary genealogical sources in terms of their value to the genealogical researcher.

The Internet provides many indexes or catalogs of primary, secondary, and tertiary information and frequently the instructions for where and how to obtain or view copies of documents and records or full-text of secondary and tertiary sources. However, very rarely is it made clear how well documented a given secondary source is, and that tertiary sources should be used with great caution. Also, when using apparently primary information from the Internet, remember that it may have been transcribed from another source—unless it was scanned. Unfortunately, it is not always easy for genealogical researchers and librarians to determine the quality of secondary and tertiary sources. Scholarly genealogical journals may help by publishing professionally researched articles verifying the validity of the primary sources used in secondary or tertiary accounts. But, generally researchers will have to check the facts themselves. Evaluation of genealogical resources on the Internet is addressed later in this part and in Activity 1.3.

A small but increasing quantity of full-text transcriptions and scanned images of documents and records are becoming available on the Internet, through the USGenWeb project (www.usgenweb.org), historical societies and libraries projects, or commercial projects such as Ancestry.com (www.ancestry.com). These genealogical reference Web sites will also be discussed in Part 2. Additional Web-based genealogical reference tools and other types of genealogical-related information are discussed in Part 2.

There are also many sites where individuals are sharing their own genealogical research data. Some of these will be discussed in Part 3 along with the genealogical communications tools and communities on the Internet in Part 3.

Planning for research travel or correspondence is made more efficient by Internet resources that identify the locations, schedules, and even the holdings of government archives, courthouses, libraries, and even cemeteries. Part 4 explores these resources in greater depth.

Are There Things the Internet Cannot Do for the Genealogical Researcher?

1. Establish direct communications with family members or fellow researchers who are not yet using the Internet, but who may have valuable information for the researcher.
2. Guarantee to have some information on every family name. If no one has published information on a given family name somewhere on the Internet, it will not be found on the Internet.
3. Guarantee the accuracy of the information found at any given location on the Internet.
4. Provide the original documents needed for documentation of genealogical research.

All of these information needs must be fulfilled by using telephones, postal mail, and travel to libraries and archives to locate and copy original or facsimile records.

The Internet is not a good first place to begin genealogical research. Genealogical research must begin offline in communication with the researcher's family. Genealogical research is best started by talking with living family members. Formal interviews or casual discussions in-person, over the telephone, or through e-mail will reveal much of the starting information needed to start looking for records and documentation on a family. Most of the records and other documentation that is required for good genealogical research will need to be obtained from archives and libraries in physical formats. Most of these information needs must be fulfilled by using telephones, postal mail, and travel to libraries and archives to locate and copy original or facsimile records and documents.

Searching on the Internet without having the initial data about names, dates of birth, marriage or death, names of mothers, brothers, grandmothers, grandfathers, etc. is going to fail. Seaching the Internet for a surname may locate some kind of information and frequently does. But how will the researcher know if it is information about their relative or ancestor if they don't have the answers to some basic questions that describe their relative or ancestor?

The basic questions genealogists have to answer are the three W's: who are you looking for, when did they live, and where did they live:

1. Who - First and last names, birth names, married names, as well as relationships—mother, father, wife, child, etc.—between individuals identified.
2. When - Birth dates, marriage dates, death dates, dates of military service, dates of events of public records (newspaper accounts, police reports, etc.).
3. Where - Places of birth, marriage, death, and other life events identified by city, town, county, township, state, province, region, etc.

The researcher will need to know these basic details about themselves and their immediate family in order to begin researching and to continue to build on their research, whether they use the Internet or not.

Prominent and respected genealogical researcher and writer Tony Burroughs describes going onto the Internet "too soon,"or before you have some of the three W's answered, as a kind of "trap":

> "There are many things beginning genealogists can do on the Internet, but I do not advocate they search for genealogical records on the Internet or other electronic technologies. I hear of too many people going to the Internet to do genealogy research without a clue about what they are looking for. They're merely name surfing without understanding the genealogical process" (2000:352).

What Hardware and Software Do I Need to Get Started?

In order to use the Internet to do any kind of research you need the basics. The researcher must first have a computer, then pay for access to the Internet, have software that sends and receives e-mail, and a Web browser to use in visiting Web sites on the Internet.

The simplest way to access the Internet is to use the computers provided by many public libraries. If the researcher needs help getting on the Internet from home, there are many books that can help. Several books that will be most useful to librarians and patrons are listed in "More Readings on Genealogical Research on the Internet." Additional books and articles will be added to the companion Web site. The researcher also might ask a friend, family member, or neighbor for their assistance and advice about local Internet providers.

How Do I Begin a Genealogical Research Project on the Internet?

Although the Internet is not a good first place to begin genealogical research, it is a good place to find guides and tutorials on how to begin genealogical research. The Internet is an excellent place to look for ideas and help in getting started on a genealogical research project.

Four of the most cited and usable beginner's genealogical research tutorial sites are discussed below. All four tutorials agree that genealogical research must begin with the individual researcher and work back from that person to their parents, grandparents, and so on. Working forward from a potential remote ancestor is very difficult. More on this concept later.

Good genealogical research begins with the individual and then branches from that person to their parents, their parent's parents, and so on. Remember the three W's discussed previously.

The four "best" beginner's genealogical research tutorials are:

1. "Getting Started: Suggestions for Beginners" National Genealogical Society (www.ngsgenealogy.org/).
2. "Guide to Tracing Family Trees" RootsWeb (http://rwguide.rootsweb.com/).
3. "How do I begin" LDS FamilySearch.org (www.familysearch.org).
4. "First Steps: Genealogy for Beginners" Lineages, Inc. (www.lineages.com/FirstSteps/).

All four tutorials clarify the basic steps for beginning research. Each presents the same steps with a different twist. This makes all four a valuable tool for librarians working to help beginners get off to a good start.

The National Genealogical Society Web site's guide to "Getting Started: Suggestions for Beginners" (www.ngsgenealogy.org/) describes the first step:

"Looking Around You . . . Identify What You Know . . .

Begin at home. Personal knowledge can form the first limbs of your family tree. First, make a simple chart, beginning with you, your parents, grandparents, and great-grandparents. Search for birth, marriage, and death certificates, and other documents that might provide names, dates, and locations. Then look at your family's Bible records, old letters, photographs and family memorabilia. Label everything you recognize. Now you are well on your way to forming the branches of your family tree—and it will begin to bud . . .

Contact family members to ask questions about their lives and those of other family members. Where did they live—what part of the country—what kind of dwelling? Did they move around while growing up? When were their relatives born; when did they die? Take along some of the old photos and attic treasures to jog their memories. And be sure to ask if you may see their old family records, letters, and memorabilia that might help you expand your search" (National Genealogical Society, 2001).

The Internet may aid this phase of the genealogical research process. E-mail makes a great communications tool for asking family members questions and clarifying the relationships of living people. If the researcher is lucky enough to find a genealogical Web site where someone related to them has posted their own genealogical data they may be able to share their information.

The RootsWeb site provides the "Guide to Tracing Family Trees," written and compiled by Julia M. Case, Rhonda McClure, and Myra Vanderpool Gormley, CG SM (http://rwguide.rootsweb.com/), which echoes and expands on the basic idea: begin with yourself and your family and then research back from there.

The genealogical research guide "How do I begin" at www.familysearch.org outlines the next steps:

"Step 1.   Identify what you know about your family.
Step 2.   Decide what you want to learn about your family.
Step 3.   Select records to search.
Step 4.   Obtain and search the record.
Step 5.   Use the information" (2001).

The Lineages, Inc. (www.lineages.com/FirstSteps/) Web site provides a tutorial "First Steps: Genealogy for Beginners" that provides a family interview "toolkit." Activity 1.2 is a simple family interview guide.

For the researcher, deciding what they want to learn about their family is a step that if thought through carefully will save problems later. A genealogical researcher may have the goal to know if their ancestors served in a particular war for a particular country, participated in a historical event, or was a ruler or member of the nobility of a particular country or region. Most of us, though, just want to know who our people are and where they came from. Genealogical researchers may want to trace their patrilineal descent—father to father to father—or their matrilineal (also called umbilical) descent—mother to mother to mother. The former relies on paternal surnames. Matrilineal descent is traced through the mother. Matrilineal descent may be more difficult to research since many historical records are incomplete in terms of women's birth names or even women's names at all. The early U.S. Federal Censuses are a problem in this sense as are some passenger lists.

For example, since I want to know about my mother's family, both patrilineal and matrilineal descent, I will begin with my mother's mother, Alice Finch (Wilson). I will trace back to her parents, Angier Wilson and Ann Wilson (Schumm) and then look both at Angier Wilson's parents, Theodore Wilson and Caroline Wilson (Lovell), as well as Ann Wilson's (Schumm) parents,

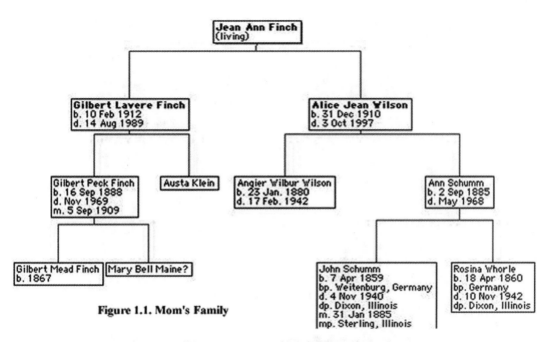

Figure 1.1. Mom's Family

Figure 1.1. Mom's Family

John Schumm and Rosina Schumm (Whorle), and so on. This tracing involves first asking my mother to recall what she knows, then locating documentation of the connections. Birth records, death records, Social Security, and other vital records all help to establish the relationships between these people and myself. Figure 1.1 is a simple family tree for my mother's family. Figure 1.2 is a photograph of John and Rosina Schumm with their two oldest children—Louis and probably Ann.

Many genealogical societies and libraries are making beginners guides available through their Web sites. Often these beginners guides are tailored for genealogical research using their local resources and focused on the research needs of their local patrons. One good example is on the Web site of the McMillan Memorial Library in Wisconsin Rapids, Wisconsin, which is also the home of the Heart O' Wisconsin Genealogical Society (www.scls.lib.wi.us/mcm/programs/genealogyconnectat.html).

You'll have an opportunity in Activity 1.1 to visit some of the Web sites that provide tutorials for beginning genealogical research and also to do some Web-based reading on the subject.

Understanding Documentation and Verification of Sources

Good genealogical research also requires documentation of the relationships between individuals. When the researcher has decided which branch of their family they want to research or which individual they'd like to learn more

Figure 1.2.   John and Rosina Schumm

about, then it's time to find information. That information will be found in a variety of different sources. Some of these sources are authoritative primary sources and some are secondary or even tertiary sources.

Documentation and verification that a genealogical connection is a fact is essential for good genealogical research. Although there are Web sites that publish some scanned images of vital records, genealogical articles, and books, the Internet does not yet provide either documentation or verification in any significant extent. It will be necessary for the researcher to write or visit archives, courthouses, genealogical organizations, and libraries to obtain verification of documentation.

"Documentary proof is not proof without analysis of the document. The fact that a secondary source is footnoted does not automatically give it the credibility of a primary source" (Stratton, 1988:96).

The National Genealogical Society Web site, www.ngsgenealogy.org, publishes a series of "Genealogical Standards and Guidelines" (www.ngsgenealogy.org/comstandards.htm), all of which are important for the researcher to be aware of when researching and communicating on the Internet. The standards and guidelines on the National Genealogical Society Web site include:

- Standards for Sound Genealogical Research
- Standards for Using Records Repositories and Libraries
- Standards for the Use of Technology in Genealogical Research
- Standards for Sharing Information with Others
- Guidelines for Publishing Web Pages on the Internet

These should be required reading for any librarian working with genealogical researchers, as well as for those genealogical researchers. In a nutshell, the first guideline document addresses the importance of documentation and integrity and is reproduced in Part 1; the second addresses respectful and careful use of materials, and appropriate interactions with librarians and archivists. The third guideline addresses the importance of thinking critically about the use of technology in research and realizing that it is a tool for research and document storage and not an end in itself. The fourth and fifth guidelines will be discussed in Part 3.

Another important reason for documenting genealogical research is to have a record of where the researcher found a certain piece of information. Take notes, use a spreadsheet or database program, and record the location, physical or Internet. By keeping track of where information is found, the researcher can find information again or tell others where they found the information. When using the Internet it may also be a good plan to record the URL of Web sites searched that failed to yield information and the dates when this was done. If the information is truly valuable, it may be a good idea to print the Web site or save it in a file.

For example, as of this writing, the Immigrant Ships Transcriber's Guild site (http://istg.rootsweb.com/) doesn't have a record for my ancestor John Schumm's arrival in the United States from Germany (around 1880) in any of the passenger lists that the group of volunteers has transcribed so far. In another example, the Illinois State Archives online archives for "Illinois State-wide Marriage Index 1763-1900" (www.cyberdriveillinois.com/departments/archives/databases.html) does not yet include Lee or Marshall County data. Because of this, I could not retrieve marriage record information for Theodore Wilson and Caroline Lovell in Palmyra Township, Lee County, Illinois (1871) or for John Engelbrecht and Anna Katrina Kapraun in Marshall County, Illi-

"Standards For Sound Genealogical Research" is reproduced with the permission of the National Genealogical Society:

"Standards For Sound Genealogical Research"
Recommended by the National Genealogical Society
Remembering always that they are engaged in a quest for truth, family history researchers consistently—

1. record the source for each item of information they collect.
2. test every hypothesis or theory against credible evidence, and reject those that are not supported by the evidence.
3. seek original records, or reproduced images of them when there is reasonable assurance they have not been altered, as the basis for their research conclusions.
4. use compilations, communications and published works, whether paper or electronic, primarily for their value as guides to locating the original records.
5. state something as a fact only when it is supported by convincing evidence, and identify the evidence when communicating the fact to others.
6. limit with words like "probable" or "possible" any statement that is based on less than convincing evidence, and state the reasons for concluding that it is probable or possible.
7. avoid misleading other researchers by either intentionally or carelessly distributing or publishing inaccurate information.
8. state carefully and honestly the results of their own research, and acknowledge all use of other researchers' work.
9. recognize the collegial nature of genealogical research by making their work available to others through publication, or by placing copies in appropriate libraries or repositories, and by welcoming critical comment.
10. consider with open minds new evidence or the comments of others on their work and the conclusions they have reached.

© 1997 by National Genealogical Society. Permission is granted to copy or publish this material provided it is reproduced in its entirety, including this notice.
Committees § Standards (*www.ngsgenealogy.org/comstandsound.htm*).

nois (around 1900). Whiteside County data is available for 1839 to 1900, so I was able to find the marriage of John Schumm to Rosina Whorle in Whiteside County as previously mentioned. The USGenWeb county project pages generally provide maps useful in identifying county names for particular time periods. For example, simple verification of the location of Palmyra Township, Lee County, Illinois can be made with any state map showing counties and townships, or historical maps from the state archives.

Librarians can only do their best to guide people to begin research with their immediate family and work backward in time, finding documentation to prove each relationship. As discussed earlier, some individuals will try to begin genealogical research with a remote ancestor and work forward in time. Generally, the only thing they know is that the potential remote ancestor has the same or similar surname or a family story holds that that person is related to the family. See "Notorious Ancestors" on Gensearcher.com (www.gensearcher.com/) for a collection of shared family stories. In *Black Roots: A Beginner's Guide to Tracing the African American Family Tree* Tony Burroughs describes this as another "trap":

> "Trap: Many novice genealogists hear they are related to some famous person a few generations back and immediately start researching that famous person. Unfortunately, many of them find out there is no connection to that person, and they've wasted years of research. So work backward; don't try to reach back and tie the person into your family. If there is some kind of connection, you'll see how it links up along the way" (2000:27).

This approach is almost always frustrating and unrewarding for both the researcher and the librarians who are trying to assist them.

For example, my paternal surname is Engelbrecht. When I was an undergraduate, a history professor pointed out to me a paragraph in the *Shorter Cambridge Medieval History*:

> "In Sweden . . . A leader appeared in the iron-mining province of Dalecarlia. This was Engelbrecht, a mine-owner, who was free from the egoism of his contemporaries, and whose far-sighted views produced a constitutional revolution. At the head of the insurgents he expelled the foreign bailiffs and forced the Council to call for 1435 a general parliament at Arboga . . . It elected Engelbrecht regent of Sweden . . . A year later Engelbrecht was murdered . . . But his ideas lived after him, and his example infected other kingdoms" (Previte-Orton, 1978:1021).

How exciting! I might be related to someone who made a difference in promoting Democracy! Other than the shared surname, I have no documentation that this Engelbrecht is in any way related to my family. At family reunions I've heard a "family story"—a tertiary source—that his son Engelbrecht Engelbrechtson went to Bavaria and that is where my family came from. I also have no documentation that the Engelbrecht of Sweden 1435 had a son or what his name was. Using the SurnameWeb (www.surnameweb.com) search tool, I located a Web site at www.users.bigpond.com/ RENGELBRECHT/Engelbrecht2.htm with a family history for the surname Engelbrecht created by an Engelbrecht living in Australia:

> "Investigations of the surname Engelbrecht or a variant show that it reappears in German documents from at least the fourteenth century when Cunrad Engelbrecht is mentioned in records in 1329 ad. Also around this time, Engelbrekt Engelbrektsson, (1390–1436) who was a mine owner of German origin, became a Swedish national hero when he led a fifteenth century rebellion against Eric of Pomerania, King of the united realms of Denmark, Norway and Sweden" (Engelbrecht, 2000).

This is very interesting, and the birth and death dates might be helpful at some point in my research, but this isn't documentation or verification of any relationship between my Engelbrecht family and those ancient Engelbrechts. Incidentally, at this writing I also have no documentation that the Engelbrecht family in Australia is any relation to my Engelbrecht family in the United States. If I were to begin my research with this Engelbrecht in 1435, or the Engelbrecht of 1329, I'd have to go back to Sweden and Germany and re-search records—written in fourteenth and fifteenth century Swedish and German, if there are any—to see who Engelbrecht's sons were (if he had any), who they married, and so on. I may end up with several hundred Engelbrecht descendants from whom I will have to trace the family name forward to the United States and my own family.

For example, in my own case, I've begun with my grandfather Joseph Engelbrecht who was born 1909 and died 1983. I searched the Social Security Death Index, free through the Ancestry.com site (www.ancestry.com), and located the index entry for his record. I printed the letter addressed to the Social Security Administration that is provided by the Ancestry.com database, and sent it along with a check. Figure 1.3 is a reproduction of the record sent to me from the Social Security Administration. It is a copy of the application filed by Grandpa Joe in order to get his Social Security number. The application copy tells me the names of Grandpa Joe's parents and confirms his birth date. Grandma Lucille told me on the telephone that they were John and Anna Engelbrecht and this application copy confirms that. I will now look for Grandpa Joe's father's records, and then his father and brothers, and then after tracing this lineage back to Germany and maybe to Sweden, I may find a relationship to the Engelbrecht of Sweden 1435.

Some individuals will not document their research or will use inappropriate documentation. As librarians, we can only guide as we have an opportunity.

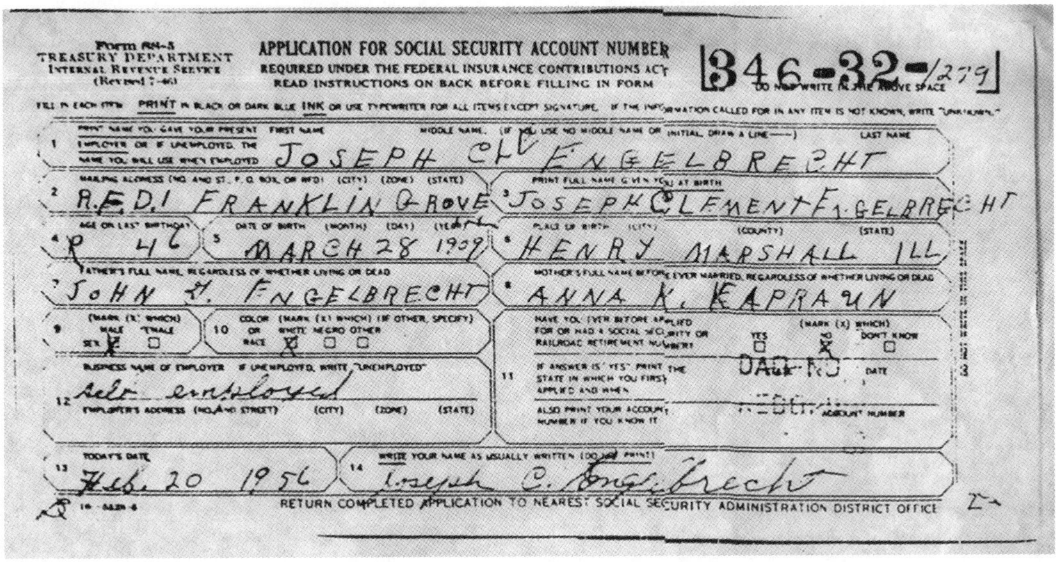

Figure 1.3. Joseph Engelbrecht Social Security Application Copy

We ourselves must have a clear idea of what constitutes good documentation.

The Internet is a source for several good documents on genealogical documentation. One of the best is "20 Ways to Avoid Genealogical Grief" by Margaret M. Sharon (www.rootsweb.com/roots-l/20ways.html) that outlines the need for and types of documentation for genealogical research. Two of the most important ways to avoid genealogical grief, in terms of using the Internet as a research tool are:

"1. Always note the source of information that you record or photocopy, and date it too. If the material is from a book, write the name, author, publisher, year of publication, ISBN or ISSN (if it has one), and also the library where you found it (or else photocopy the title page). Occasionally you'll find that you need to refer to a book again, or go back to great aunt Matilda to clarify something she told you" (Sharon, 1995).

And also

"8. Remember that just because information is on computer or in print, it ain't necessarily fact! Information in recent family histories is often based on that from older published works. If the older books are incorrect, the wrong information simply gets repeated and further disseminated" (Sharon, 1995).

The latter way to "Avoid Genealogical Grief" introduces our next topic.

Location: http://www.cyberdriveillinois.com/cgi-bin/archives/marriage.s

Illinois Statewide Marriage Index 1763 - 1900

Click here for information about how to obtain copies of original marriage records.

GROOM	BRIDE	CNTY	DATE	VOL/PAGE	LIC
SCHUMM, JOHN	WOHRLE, ROSE		WHITESIDE	01/31/1885 /	00006549

Figure 1.4.   John Schumm and Rosina Whorle Marriage License Search Result from the Illinois Statewide Marriage Index 1763-1900

How Do I Evaluate Genealogical Data on the Internet and Verify Sources?

Many people are under the impression that there is a lot of genealogical stuff on the Internet, and they are right.

There is a lot of just stuff on the Internet that is related to genealogical research. There is no overall quality control for genealogical research materials on the Internet. Some sites will be well-documented and accurately compiled and others will be little more than family fantasies.

Some full-text collections will be scanned records images and professionally verified indexing, and some sites will be just junk that someone made up. There is also a lot in between. Many sites contain vital records indexing compiled by volunteers, hand-copied cemetery and other records, and many individually compiled family trees that are of very high and reliable quality.

As long as we keep the problems in mind, the benefits of using the Internet as a tool for genealogical research are great.

The problems with genealogical information obtained from the Internet are typical of all information obtained from the Internet. Basically in order of the most frequent occurrence the problems include:

1. Typos
2. Factual errors (accidental or deliberate)
3. Opinion stated as fact
4. Out-of-date information
5. Bias
6. Deliberate fraud

Human transcription or copying of records frequently results in minor or sometimes major errors. For example, in the transcriptions in the Illinois State Archives Internet database for "Illinois State-wide Marriage Index 1763-1900"

Figure 1.5. **Transcription of Newpaper Obituary Clipping from *Dixon Evening Telegraph* for Mrs. Rosina Schumm (Whorle)**

Dixon Evening Telegraph – OBITUARY

Mrs. Rosina Schumm

Mrs. Rosina Schumm (nee Whorle) was born in Germany on April 18, 1860 and passed from this life in her home at 510 Squires avenue, Dixon, Ill., on Tuesday, Nov. 10, 1942, at the age of 82 years, 6 months and 23 days.

Mrs. Schumm came to America at the age of 21 years and was united in marriage to John Schumm in Sterling soon after arrival in this country. They made their home in Sterling until 1894, in Clinton Iowa, until 1900 and in Dixon subsequently.

Mr. And Mrs. Schumm joined the Evangelical church of Sterling in 1888 on confession of faith. They transferred their membership to the Evangelical church in Clinton during the years of their residence there. On March 28, 1900 they affiliated with the Grace Evangelical church of Dixon and of which church they have been faithful and devoted members through these many years. Mr. Schumm preceded her in death on Nov. 4, 1940 and notwith-standing the thoughtful care with which her family surrounded her since his passing, she missed his companionship very much. However, she grew old beautifully in the something of the spirit of the poet who wrote:
"Grow old along with me?
The best is yet to be,
The last of life, for which the
   First was made:
Our times are in His hand
Who saith "A whole I planned,
Youth shows but half trust God;
   See all nor be afraid."
   —(Browning)

Left to mourn her passing are the following: one son, Louis of Dixon; five daughters, Mrs. Mary Prescott, Mrs. Anna Wilson, and Mrs. Harriett Finch of Dixon; Mrs. Emma DeCamp of LaGrange, Ill.; and Mrs. Elsie Dunne of Stock-ton, Calif.

Funeral services were held on Friday, November 13, 1942 from the home and the Grace Evangelical church of Dixon, Rev. George D. Nielsen, pastor, offi-ciating. Interment in Oakwood.

Figure 1.6.   1900 Census Data for Gilbert M and Helen J. Finch Amboy Township. Lee County, Illinois

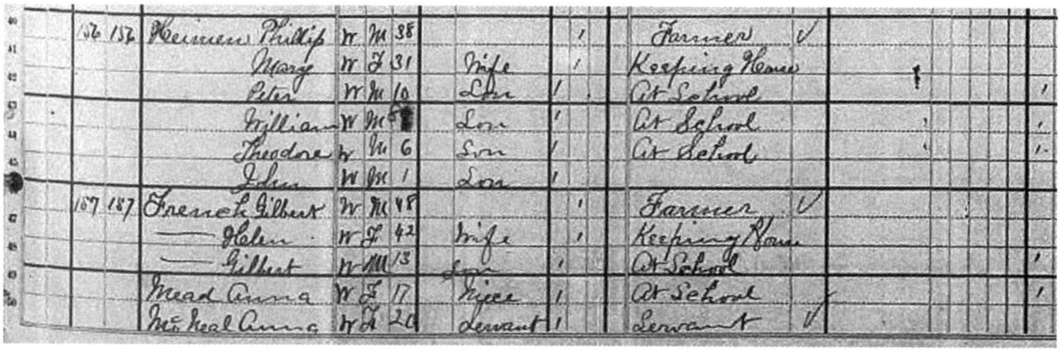

Figure 1.7.   1880 Census Data for Gilbert M and Helen J. Finch Amboy Township. Lee County, Illinois

at www.cyberdriveillinois.com/departments/archives/databases.html, the entry for the marriage of John Schumm to Rosina Whorle vol/page 01/31/1885 license 00006549 in Whiteside County, Illinois, has recorded Rosina's name as WOHRLE (Figure 1.4). The 1885 marriage data contradicts data from her 1942 obituary in the *Dixon Evening Telegraph* (Figure 1.5) that stated her birthname as Whorle.

Another problem is misspellings or typos by clerks, census takers, registrars, or others recording vital information. For example, Gilbert M. Finch and his wife Helen J. (Mead) are listed correctly on the scanned image of the 1900 Census data sheet for Amboy Township, Lee County Illinois (Figure 1.6). On the 1880 Census data sheet, however, they are listed as Gilbert M and Helen J "French" (Figure 1.7).

A photocopy of Rosina and John's original marriage record can be ordered from Whiteside County Clerk's Office and the spelling and dates can be checked from the copy of the original. The Web site "Vital Records Information" at www.vitalrec.com contains information about how and where to order particular vital records from counties and states in the United States, as well as Canada and other countries. We'll see this site again in Part 2. In the case of the Finch/French alteration, the first names, dates and places of birth, match between the 1880 and 1900 Census images so we can have some assurance that the records refer to the same Finch family.

One of the most valuable sources of information on the Internet is also the most vulnerable to accidental or deliberate error. This is the provision by fellow genealogical researchers of their own family history and genealogical data via their Web sites. These Web sites can be an outstanding source of valuable information for you and your patrons or they may be misleading at best and deliberately fraudulent at worst.

For example, during an in-person genealogical research on the Internet workshop one of my students found her own data listed through a Gendex (www.gendex.com) indexed Web site. She was able to discover the name and e-mail address of the person providing the information. He was contacted and asked two things: remove her information from public view since she was obviously living and correct her mother's name (person had listed her aunt as her mother). Since both her aunt and her mother are still living she requested that the information also be removed from the public Web.

Publishing vital information about living individuals on the Web is a very bad idea. Most guidelines for publishing genealogy on the Web recommend that information about living individuals be omitted or modified to a place-holder such as "living spouse." Identity thieves need only a name and a birth date to apply for credit or identification cards. Privacy and security guidelines for publishing genealogical information on the Web are discussed further in Part 2.

There are individuals and organizations that do try to maintain a certain measure of quality control and reporting of truly "bad" information on Web sites. Foremost among these are Cyndi's List (www.cyndislist.com) and RootsWeb (www.rootsweb.com). In Activity 1.3 you'll have an opportunity to visit some additional quality control sites and do some Web-based reading on the subject.

The questions that must be asked about every genealogical Web site are:

1. Who provided the information?
2. Does the information provider provide evidence of documentation that supports the information provided?
3. What original document or documents is a Web-based database based on? And was it transcribed or scanned and by whom?

If a thorough reading through the Web site doesn't answer all three of these questions easily then the information is not usable as documentation of genealogical research. If the researcher really must use the information, then the site should at least be able to answer question number one. The best strategy is to contact the information provider to ask them to provide documentation in support of the information they are providing, or a detailed description of the source documents for any databases they are providing.

"In the final analysis, good standards come down to an admixture of common sense and a decent knowledge of the specialized subject matter. In genealogy it is important to know not just what was said, but who said it. And then we must ask: How did the person saying it know? This is a seemingly simple concept, but there are many people who have a mental block when it comes to accepting it. That is usually because they have been brought up to believe that if it is in print, it must be true. Therefore they see no need to go behind any assertion that appears in print" (Stratton, 1988:45).

Genealogical research is an enjoyable and frequently rewarding pursuit. Successful researchers begin with their own immediate family and work back in time to document connections to their ancestors. Good genealogical research using any information medium requires solid research and verifiable documentation. Genealogical research using the Internet may require some additional thought and attention to documentation because of the sheer quantity of information, the nature of some of the information, and the need to verify the source of the information found on the Internet. The convenience, efficiency of information retrieval, and the communications networking with other researchers and family members counter-balances that extra effort to obtain and verify documentation for genealogical research data.

How Should Librarians and Researchers Conduct a Genealogy Reference Interview?

Genealogical researchers may present the library reference desk staff with some challenging reference interviews. Genealogical researchers:

1. May not share the specific family information required for the librarian to be able to address their questions successfully.
2. May not have or be able to share the specific family information needed to address their questions successfully.
3. May share more of their family data than the librarian needs to answer their question.
4. May share sensitive family information in regard to medical history and criminal or scandalous activity of their ancestors or living family members.
5. May be unhappy if the library staff disproves or cannot prove the "truth" of a "family story" or legend, or of an illustrious or infamous ancestral connection.

Success Story 1.1
Using Old-Fashioned Research Methods with Web-Based Information Technology

James Swan jswan@ckls.org (Author of *The Librarian's Guide to Genealogical Research*)

In the 1960s my grandmother, Olive Elizabeth Moore, went to Wisconsin to search for her ancestors. She died in 1979, before she could go over with me the genealogy she had gathered. Handwritten notes, pedigree charts, and photocopies with little or no source documentation typified most of the data I inherited.

All of this information languished untouched in my "genealogy briefcase" until 1991 when I bought my first computer and installed Personal Ancestral File™ 2.0. I entered all of the data I had into PAF and started again to do research. At about the same time a Family History Center™ was established in our town, making it much easier to access the resources of the Family History Library™. From 1991 to 1999 I had all but ignored the Ridgeway line, checking occasionally for Joseph Ridgeway in some of the electronic databases I could access.

After eight years it was time to work on the Ridgeway line. It would mean tackling more difficult research. In 1999 the Familysearch.org Web site became available on the Internet, making it even easier to access FamilySearch™ databases and the Family History Library Catalog™. Even though I made one trip to Kansas City, Missouri to check out the regional resources of the National Archives and Records Administration, I could have done all of the research I describe in this article without leaving town. What I found turned out to be rewarding beyond belief. Coupling the latest advances in technology with plain old letter writing, I was able to crack a brick wall. At least I had been unable to find anything on my Ridgeway line after years staring at the names on my pedigree chart and not knowing where to look.

When I first decided to concentrate my research on Florence Ridgeway the only firm data I had was her marriage certificate. It gave the date of their marriage, her husband's name, and his parents. It gave her Florence's father as Joseph Ridgeway and her mother as Poley Ridgeway. The marriage occurred in Fond du Lac County, Wisconsin. I also knew that Florence had died soon after the birth of her daughter Harriet Warden, my grandmother's mother. That is all the Ridgeway data I could glean from my grandmother's genealogy.

I started my research by checking all of the online databases I could find, including Ancestry.com™ and Familysearch.org™. Nothing I found helped me extend my line or connect with the research of others. I found a pre-1907 death index for Wisconsin in the Family History Library Catalog. I ordered the microfiche set through my local Family History Center and found exact death dates for a Joseph Ridgeway and Mary Jane Ridgeway in Fond du Lac, Wisconsin. This was enough information to order death certificates for these individuals.

The next step was to check the *Handybook for Genealogists* to learn how to get copies of the death records. Under Fond du Lac County, Wisconsin, I found the address and telephone number for the Register of Deeds and a listing of the records they had. I called them and asked for forms and pricing to request copies of death certificates. After the forms came I sent for copies of the death certificates for Joseph Ridgeway and his wife. Copies of the records cost $7.00 each and came back within 10 days. Death certificates can contain a lot of information of value to genealogists, but the information is not always reliable because the person who provided the information was not present when most of the events occurred. The only information you can count on to be absolutely accurate is the date of death and the location. Everything else is secondhand information and needs to be verified, but it can provide valuable clues for further research.

This is what I gleaned from Joseph Ridgeway's death certificate:

Full name: Joseph Ridgeway
Birth date: 1 August 1831
Place of birth: England
Death date: 27 January 1899
Place of death: Fond du Lac, Fond du Lac, Wisconsin
Age: 67 years, 5 months, 26 days
Occupation: File manufacturer
Father: William Ridgeway
Father's birthplace: England
Mother: Elizabeth (Ashton) Ridgeway
Mother's birthplace: England
Name of Spouse: Mary Jane (Stinson) Ridgeway
Residence: 114 W. Division, Fond du Lac
Burial: Rienzi Cemetery

This is what I gleaned from Mary Jane Ridgeway's death certificate:

Maiden name: Mary Jane Stinson
Birth date: 17 April 1825
Place of birth: Clinton, Maine
Death date: 10 May 1900
Place of death: Fond du Lac, Fond du Lac, Wisconsin

Age: 75 years 23 days
Father: Isaac Stinson
Father's birthplace: Litchfield, Maine
Mother: Harriet Wardwell
Mother's birthplace: Frankfort, Maine
Name of Spouse: Joseph Ridgeway (deceased)
Residence: 114 W. Division, Fond du Lac, Wisconsin
Burial: Rienzi Cemetery

These two death certificates gave me more leads than I could check out in several weeks. The only serious discrepancy was in the spelling of Mary Jane Stinson's mother's maiden name. I am still trying to find out the correct spelling.

Armed with exact death dates, I called the Fond du Lac (Wisconsin) Public Library and asked them to look up obituaries for Joseph and Mary Jane Ridgeway. They found the obituaries, made copies, and sent them to me along with a bill for $2.83. I sent them a check and a thank you note right away.

The obituary for Mary Jane Stinson Ridgeway had little if any additional genealogical information.

Here is what I gleaned from the obituary for Joseph Ridgeway:

Birthplace: Manchester, England
Death date: 27 January 1899
Residence: 114 W. Division, Fond du Lac, Wisconsin
He resided in Fond du Lac, Wisconsin for more than 30 years.
Children: Joseph H. Ridgeway
     William of California
     Mrs. Morris of California

I was on a roll, so I contacted the Probate Office in Fond du Lac County. They charged $4.00 to search for the probate record and $1.00 for each page they copied. After the search they sent me an e-mail message informing me that they had four pages with genealogical information. I sent them a check for $4.00 and they sent me the pages.

Here is what I gleaned.
Addresses for two of the heirs:

William J. Ridgeway, 14 Hill Street, San Francisco, California
Lottie Morris, Modesto, California
Another heir: Harriet Moore. [Even though her mother Florence (Ridgeway) Warden had died, Harriet (Warden) Moore was married at the time of probate and was named as an heir.]

From this information I was able to check a California death index and find death certificates for two of Florence Ridgeway's siblings. While I was at the National Archives in Kansas City I found the 1870 census record for the family of Joseph and Mary Jane Ridgeway. This could have been a beginning step, but it turned out to be one of the later steps. Without using an index I found the family in about 30 minutes.

Here is what I found.

City: Fond du Lac   County: Fond du Lac   State: Wisconsin

Name	Age	Sex	Color	Trade	Birthplace
Ridgeway, Joseph	39	M	W	Filemaker	England
Mary	40	F	W	At home	Maine
Florence	20	F	W	At home	Mass.
Lotty E.	16	F	W	At home	do
William J.	11	M	W		St. John, N.B.
Joseph H.	9	M	W		St. John, N.B.

The next step was to verify the information for the parents Joseph Ridgeway and Mary Jane Stinson. I started by searching for William Ridgeway as the father of Joseph Ridgeway on Familysearch.org. I found an International Genealogical Index™ (IGI) record that was a christening record that had been extracted from church records at Cathedral, Manchester, Lancashire, England. The christening had occurred 21 days after the birth of Joseph Ridgeway. I tried a marriage search for William Ridgeway and Elizabeth Ashton and found they were married 21 February 1831. I did a parent search and found the siblings of Joseph, all christened at Cathedral, Manchester, Lancashire, England. By clicking on the film number under the Source I was able to get the film number from which the church records had been extracted. I ordered the film through my local Family History Center and was able to verify the data from the original sources. I have now been able to extend the genealogy of Florence Ridgeway back four generations on the Ridgeway side.

That left the Stinson line to check out. The death certificate for Mary Jane Stinson said that her father was born in Litchfield, Maine, but my road atlas did not show a Litchfield, Maine. I had heard of Litchfield, Connecticut, and thought someone had made a mistake on the death certificate. I went to the online version of the Family History Library Catalog and did a Place Search. I typed in Litchfield as part of Maine and found that Litchfield was in Kennebec County, Maine. I clicked on Display Topics and found the films for Litchfield, Maine available from the Family History Library. I also checked for Frankfort, Maine and found out it is located in Waldo County. Because Mary Jane Stinson was born in Clinton, Maine I ordered a film from the Family History Library on the town records of Clinton. The record had a marriage record for Isaac Stinson and Harriet Wardsworth. They were married in Clinton, Kennebec, 1 February 1823, which fit the profile for the family.

I also checked Familysearch.org for Isaac Stinson and found an IGI record for the marriage that matched the marriage in the town record. I also found an Ancestral File record that had been submitted by Neva Strever in 1983. I wanted to contact her but could not find a current address so I checked the Social Security Death Index™, which is online through Ancestry.com. She had died since submitting the Stinson record to the Ancestral File™. The IGI Record was an extracted record and I was able to do a parent search and find the children of Isaac and Harriet Stinson.

Not willing to lose the momentum I was enjoying, I went to Rootsweb.com to find out if there were any mailing lists that I could join. Maybe I could find other genealogists who were working on my lines and could share what they had with me. I subscribed to the Stinson mailing list, the Kennebec, Maine mailing list, and the Waldo, Maine, mailing list. I sent queries right away and was very encouraged by the responses. One Stinson researcher sent me a large envelope containing 20 pages of Stinson data. Another Stinson list member sent me an e-mail that gave me the marriage of Joseph Ridgeway and Mary Jane Stinson in Lowell, Middlesex, Massachusetts. Also the census index on Ancestry.com led me to an 1850 census record for Joseph Ridgeway in Lowell, Massachusetts.

Not all of the sources I checked produced a good result. Some were dead ends, and I chose not to bore you with the details of looking in places that didn't have anything that could help me. I ordered the 1895 Wisconsin State census from Heritage Quest™ through my public library, but it only listed the heads of households and the number of persons in the home. I thought about checking naturalization and immigration records for Joseph Ridgeway, but I didn't need to because of the completeness of the IGI record from Manchester, England.

I still haven't followed up on all the leads I have on the ancestors of Florence Ridgeway. Checking all of the church records in Manchester, England could take several months or even years. These records go back to the 1600s. The Stinson line in Maine goes back several generations and then over to Ireland. I need to check Lowell, Massachusetts for the birth of Florence Ridgeway and her sister Lottie. I need to check the records of St. John, New Brunswick, Canada for the two younger brothers. I still need to find a birth record for Harriet Warden Moore, the only child of Florence Ridgeway.

I was hoping to find a connection on the Ancestral File, Genserv.com™, or the Ancestry World Tree™ on Ancestry.com that would take me back ten generations, but so far I haven't been that lucky. I have found more information than I had ever hoped to find just six months ago.

Reference interview techniques that are successful with any other reference questions will be useful in working with genealogical researchers. The classic advice for successful reference interviews from the classic text *Introduction to Reference Work* is:

"The path to success is a calm Zen-like attitude. This is based as much upon a good disposition as confidence in when to say, ever so politely 'Let's see what we can find.' Work in a reference area will point the way. Reference sources inevitably will disclose answers to even the most remote, difficult query. And if not a precise response, at least it will be a reply which will satisfy" (Katz, 2001:25).

The genealogical researcher may be asking any of the basic types of reference questions: known item, directional, ready-reference, specific-search, or research. Good knowledge of the local collection, shared databases, as well as what might be available on the Internet along with a careful reference interview will suffice for most genealogy reference questions. As Katz tells us "The reference interview has several objectives. The first is to find out what and how much data the user needs" (2001:19).

Here are some additional ideas for reference interviews with genealogy researchers:

> If the genealogical researcher will not share information required to answer the question, a calm and pleasant response to the researcher that without the information it will be difficult to answer the question and then show them the resources that are available for them to use themselves. Provide instruction on how to use the resource if needed. For example, one researcher I worked with who approached me with "I need a death certificate for my grandfather." I asked her for her grandfather's first and last name, and where he had lived at the time of his death. She replied that she just wanted me to tell her how to get death records. She was clearly reluctant to tell me her grandfather's name. I did not push the issue in any way. I showed her the Social Security Death Records (SSDI) database through RootsWeb (www.rootsweb.com) and the Vital Records Web site (www.vitalrec.com). She didn't require any instruction.

If the genealogical researcher simply does not have specific family information needed to address their question successfully, then back up and work on the question of finding that information first. Always offer constructive options. For example, a researcher wanted to know if her great-grandfather had come from Ireland. Her father's and grandfather's last name was Regan. Both were named William. She did not know her great-grandfather's first name but thought it might have been Patrick and that his last name might have been O'Regan. She also did not know when he might have come to the U.S. A search of the Ellis Island Records database (www.ellisisland.org) retrieves more than a hundred Patrick Regans and a more manageable number of Patrick O'Regans. In order to discern which of these immigrants might be her great-grandfather she needed more data. Our conclusion was that she obtain her grandfather's birth certificate from the appropriate organization and hope that that record contained her great-grandfather's given and surnames and an approximate idea of when he arrived in the U.S.

Sharing family information is a hallmark of the genealogical researcher. Most of us are so interested in our own research that we sometimes don't stop to think if someone else is really all that interested. Many reference staff enjoy hearing about other people's family research. However, there are times when the reference desk is too busy to spend much time. Simple courtesy in asking the researcher to come back when the desk is less busy is usually all that is needed. If the information being shared is very personal the situation may be more difficult to manage. This is the time when the "calm Zen-like attitude" can help. A courteous re-direction of the researcher to their actual information needs generally suffices. Be careful not to be judgmental or to give advice. For example, one researcher insisted on sharing with me that his ancestor had killed a certain number of "Yankees." Since my ancestors were all "Yankees" I might have been offended. I re-directed the interview by asking what additional information the researcher needed, if any, related to that ancestor. If the researcher is talking about family medical history an appropriate response may be "You might want to consult a medical professional about that." On one occasion a researcher was very interested in the genetic diseases associated with first cousin marriages. I was able to refer her to a medical text and to locate the phone number and address of a genetic counselor.

Occasionally, a genealogy researcher will be upset about the results of their research, especially if the records do not support a family story or relationship with an illustrious or infamous ancestor. It has never happened to me that a researcher I worked with did get upset. Rather, they seemed to either be philosophical about the research results or they dismissed the records as being "incomplete" or not accurate in some way. A non-judgmental response can keep the situation from becoming unpleasant. Never, never, say, "I told you so" or insist to the researcher that the records are right and they are wrong. After all, where is the harm if someone wants to believe in their own family story or illustrious connection.

Success Story 1.2
The Challenges of Interviewing Genealogical Researchers

Deborah Keener deb.keener@wayne.lib.oh.us, Head of Genealogy and Local History, Wayne County Public Library

Trying to figure out what exactly the researcher is looking for is the biggest hurdle to jump. Several months ago, I had an older woman come in to the library and she wanted information on the Kelley family. From her attitude, I could tell she was not a serious researcher. She expected me to pull off of our shelf her entire family history. She knew little about the Kelley family and I was not sure she was related. She had mentioned that her son had traced the Kelleys somewhere near Columbus, or so she thought. I finally pulled that bit of information from her. She did not have a five-generation chart with her, nor did she have family group sheets, nor did she have any notes. Through a series of questions, she finally mentioned she was interested in Gemimah Kelley and she mentioned the Stauffer Cemetery. Things began to click in my mind. I had been in contact with an individual who was trying to restore the Stauffer family cemetery and had run into problems with the farmer owning the adjacent property. After she permitted the words Stauffer Cemetery to slip through her lips, I knew that sure enough she was not truly interested in doing genealogy research on the Kelley family. She wanted to prove that the Cemetery did not belong to the Stauffer family, that it was the property of the Kelley family. Since no living Gemimah Kelley family members could be found, then the cemetery could be considered abandoned, and her son could proceed to destroy the cemetery to use it as farmland (less than 0.5 acres). A month later, I found out that this woman who originally came to the library looking for the Kelley family, had filed suit against the coordinator of the Stauffer Family Cemetery restoration group and all of the deceased heirs of Samuel Stauffer who are buried in the cemetery. It hasn't gone to court, yet, but the story made the local news.

So to get back to the original question, it is very helpful if researchers come to the library with a generational chart completed to the best of the researcher's ability. Even if a chart has not been completed, it is helpful if the researchers have notes including names and approximate dates of those ancestors being researched. At least this will give staff a clue to whether we need to be searching in the eighteenth, nineteenth, twentieth, or twenty-first century. And it is true—sometimes we have traveled through all four centuries in one day's time.

It is also helpful to know the intentions of the researchers. Are they researching to publish family information? Are they researching their family history to disprove or prove family lore? Are they researching for health or legal reasons? How far back do they want to go? Do they want to stick only with the direct line and ignore all collateral lines? (We actually discourage this practice because many times you find information on your direct ancestor through information on collateral lines.) Does the researcher want to trace the adopted line and/or their biological line?

Has the researcher already been in contact with older relatives who may be able to provide insight into the family? Are there any known older relatives who would be willing and able to help?

Are you trying to do research in the county or surrounding counties, in the state, out of state, or out of the country?

If it is children or young adults coming in, it helps to know if it is for Cub Scouts, for a school project, for 4-H, etc. If it is for a school project, what criteria did the teacher set?

I could go on and on. As staff members, we have to look at each case individually and not be afraid to interact and try to get into the researcher's family to gain a better understanding on how to direct the researcher further.

References

The American Heritage Dictionary of the English Language, Third Edition. 1996, 1992. New York: Houghton Mifflin Company.

Burroughs, T. 2001. *Black Roots: A Beginners Guide to Tracing the African American Family Tree*. New York: Simon and Schuster.

Engelbrecht, R. 2000. [Online]. Available: www.users.bigpond.com/RENGELBRECHT/Engelbrecht2.htm [2001, October 22].

Family Search. 2001. "How Do I Begin" [Online]. Available: www.familysearch.org [2001, October 22].

George, A. 1997. *Murder Runs in the Family*. New York: Avon Books.

Katz, W. 2001. *Introduction to Reference Work, Vol. 1*. New York: McGraw-Hill.

National Geographic Society. 2001. [Online]. Available: www.ngsgenealogy.org [2001, October 22].

Previte-Orton, C.W. 1978. *The Shorter Cambridge Medieval History*. Cambridge: Cambridge University Press.

Sharon, Margaret M. 1995. *20 Ways to Avoid Genealogical Grief* [Online]. Available: www.rootsweb.com/roots-1/20ways.html [2001, October 22].

Stratton, E.A. 1988. *Applied Genealogy*. Salt Lake City, Utah: Ancestory Inc.

Activity 1.1. Beginning a Family History Project

Overview:

In this Activity you'll have an opportunity to visit some good Web sites that provide tutorials for beginning genealogical researchers. Visit each site and answer the following questions about each site:

1. Who provides this Web site (What organization or person(s))?
2. Why is this Web site being provided?
3. What is the first step for genealogical research described by this Web site?
4. What does the tutorial recommend that you use the Internet for in doing your genealogical research?

"20 Ways to Avoid Genealogical Grief"

http://www.rootsweb.com/roots-l/20ways.html

"How Do I Begin?"

http://www.familysearch.org/Eng/Search/RG/guide/all_t3_resmeth_-_how_do_i_begin.asp

"Getting Started"

http://www.ngsgenealogy.org/getstart/body_frame.html
Immigration and Ships Passenger Lists Research Guide
http://home.att.net/~arnielang/shipgide.html
RootsWeb Guide
http://www.rootsweb.com/~rwguide/

"Learning about Genealogy and the Internet"

http://www.scls.lib.wi.us/mcm/programs/genealogyconnectat.html
Note: This is a special example representing hundreds of similar sites offered by regional and local genealogical societies and libraries.
Note: If you are working self-paced and would like instructor feedback e-mail your responses and questions to *diane@kovacs.com.*

Activity 1.2. Establishing What You Know and What You Need to Know About Your Family

Overview:

In this activity you will answer some basic starting questions about the family you are interested in researching. These basic questions are important for continuing your research and effectively using the tools and techniques discussed in the rest of this book/workshop.

STEP 1

Answer these questions as well as you are able. Answer the questions using facts from your own family or the family of a patron, friend, or other person that you are working with.

1. What is your first, middle, last name (surname)?
2. When were you born? (month/day/year and time) List all of the information that you know.
3. Where were you born? (city, county, state, province, country, township) List all of the information that you know.
4. What is your father's first, middle, last name (surname)?
5. When was your father born? (month/day/year and time) List all of the information that you know.
6. Where was your father born? (city, county, state, province, country, township) List all of the information that you know.
7. What is your mother's first, middle, birth name (surname she was born with)?
8. When was your mother born? (month/day/year and time) List all of the information that you know.
9. Where was your mother born? (city, county, state, province, country, township) List all of the information that you know.
10. What was your father's father's (paternal grandfather's) name? (first, middle, surname)
11. When was your father's father born? (month/day/year and time) List all of the information that you know.
12. Where was your father's father born? (city, county, state, province, country, township) List all of the information that you know.
13. What was your father's mother's (grandmother's) name? (first, middle, birth surname [surname she was born with])
14. When was your father's mother born? (month/day/year and time) List all of the information that you know.
15. Where was your father's mother born? (city, county, state, province, country, township) List all of the information that you know.

16. What was your mother's father's (maternal grandfather's) name? (first, middle, surname)
17. When was your mother's father born? (month/day/year and time) List all of the information that you know.
18. Where was your mother's father born? (city, county, state, province, country, township) List all of the information that you know.
19. What was your mother's mother's (maternal grandmother's) name? (first, middle, birth surname [surname she was born with])
20. When was your mother's mother born? (month/day/year and time) List all of the information that you know.
21. Where was your father's mother born? (city, county, state, province, country, township) List all of the information that you know.
22. Do you have brother(s) or sister(s)? If you do what are your sibling(s)' first, middle, last names (surnames)?
23. Does your mother have brother(s) or sister(s)? If she does, what are her sibling(s)' first, middle, last names (surnames)?
24. Does your father have brother(s) or sister(s)? If he does, what are his sibling(s)' first, middle, last names (surnames)?
25. Did your maternal grandfather have brother(s) or sister(s)? If he did, what are his sibling(s)' first, middle, last names (surnames)?
26. Did your maternal grandmother have brother(s) or sister(s)? If she did, what are her sibling(s)' first, middle, last names (surnames)?
27. Did your paternal grandfather have brother(s) or sister(s)? If he did, what are his sibling(s)' first, middle, last names (surnames)?
28. Did your paternal grandmother have brother(s) or sister(s)? If she did, what are her sibling(s)' first, middle, last names (surnames)?

STEP 2

Which questions above were you unable to answer?

STEP 3

What documentation/verification do you have for the answers you were able to respond to? (e.g., birth certificates, census records, Social Security death record, interviewed the person on a particular date, interviewed your parent on a particular date)

STEP 4

These questions and their answers, as well as the questions you still need to ask will form the starting point for your genealogical research.
Note: If you are working self-paced and would like instructor feedback e-mail your responses and questions to *diane@kovacs.com*.

Activity 1.3. Evaluating Genealogical Data Published on the Internet and Verifying Sources

Overview:

In this activity you'll have an opportunity to visit some Web sites where responsible volunteer genealogical researchers have collected and exposed "bad" genealogical information on the Internet. In addition, links are provided to two excellent articles discussing this problem on the Internet.

STEP 1

Begin by connecting to the following articles and reading them online (If these links seem to have moved, look through the archives at the *Ancestry Daily News* main site *http://www.ancestry.com/library/view/news/articles/ d_p_1_archive.asp* to locate the current URL).
Morgan, G.G. 2001. "Bogus Genealogies." *Ancestry Daily News.* 1/19/2001. *http://www.ancestry.com/library/view/news/articles/3224.asp*
Neil, M.J. 2001. "It's on 1,000 Web Sites." *Ancestry Daily News.* 1/17/2001. *http://www.ancestry.com/library/view/news/articles/3202.asp*

STEP 2

Visit each of the following sites and answer these questions about each site (on the workshop Web site there are Web forms to report your responses for instructor feedback):

1. Who sponsors or provides this information?
2. What are the qualifications of the organization or person(s) who are exposing the "bad" information sites on the Internet?
3. What is the motivation of the organization or person(s) who are exposing the "bad" information sites?
4. What "bad" information site seems to you the most dangerous or horrifying in terms of your own or your patrons' genealogical research?

Ancestor Detective Genealogical Web Site Watchdog
http://www.ancestordetective.com/watchdog.htm

Cyndi's List Category: Myths, Hoaxes, and Scams
http://www.CyndisList.com/myths.htm
Note: Read through the information under the sub-categories: Common Genealogical Myths, as well as Other Myths, Hoaxes, & Scams

International Black Sheep Society of Genealogists Hall of Shame
http://blacksheep.rootsweb.com/shame.html
Note: Page down until you see the list of "bad" Web sites or Web sites where problems have been reported.

Genealogy Fraud/Fraudulent Lineages
http://www.linkline.com/personal/xymox/fraud/fraud.htm
Note: The parent site for this page is America's First Families Online Genealogical Society for 1600's Ancestors *http://www.linkline.com/personal/xymox/index.htm.*
Note: If you are working self-paced and would like instructor feedback e-mail your responses and questions to *diane@kovacs.com.*

Part 2
How to Find and Use Basic Genealogical Reference and Documentation Tools on the Web

---

"Why Genealogists Love the Internet

If there is one thing genealogists love more than cemeteries, it is libraries. <grin> The Internet has been called the world's largest library and with good reason. The Net makes a world of resources available to genealogists twenty-four hours per day at very reasonable costs. Most resources for genealogists on the Internet are free" (Renick and Wilson, 1999:7).

This part discusses the selection of indispensable high-quality genealogical reference sources on the Web.

The Ten Best Genealogical Reference and Documentation Tools on the Web

Once a research question has been defined, the first step is usually to gather information for further research by using appropriate reference tools. Genealogical research on the Internet is no exception. Before looking for genealogical reference tools, you or your patron should have already:

1. Established an interest in family history or genealogy.
2. Decided how far back in time and how broadly across the researcher's family tree they wish to research.
3. Written down what is already known about the family including notes on supporting documentation.
4. Interviewed living relatives and recorded the information that they've provided.

At this stage, the researcher is ready to find and use genealogical reference tools to help pursue additional data, documentation, and verification of their family genealogical data. A genealogical reference tool is a source of information that will help the researcher find additional information or provide primary data. On the Internet, there are several types of genealogical reference tools. The following is an outline of these types:

- Personal Family History Pages
- Searchable Databases of Personal Family History Pages
- Classified Directories and Collections of Internet Genealogical Resources (Metasites)
- Searchable Indexes for Commercially Collected Data Products
- Searchable Indexes for Government Collected Data Products
- Indexes to Physical Resources

Personal Family History Pages are the most numerous. Most offer basic genealogical data, such as the dates of birth, marriage, death, or other vital events. Other genealogy reference Web sites are known as metasites. Metasites are collections of Web site links, sometimes searchable, often browseable, often organized by subject areas or types of information. Searchable generally means you can type in a keyword and retrieve a list of items from the database. Browseable means you can look through the subject headings and scan for individual links that look interesting. Genealogical metasites are used to locate additional Web sites that may provide or help to locate basic genealogical data. For example, an individual Web site would provide an index or ordering information for vital records for a single county, but a metasite would link you to all the vital records information Web sites on the Internet.

There are also some Web sites that provide searchable indexes to commercially or government-compiled data or records. Some of these genealogy reference Web sites also provide access to full-text transcriptions or scanned images of genealogical information. Some genealogical reference tools on the Internet are indexes to physical resources, e.g., microfilms or CD-ROMs. Others are full-text materials of varying quality and type, published on the Web through the efforts of genealogical researchers. Some metasites not only organize genealogical Web sites, they also review and annotate sources of genealogical information on the Web. Some of the genealogical data sources on the Web provide either transcriptions or scanned images of genealogical documentation and records.

Although the Internet is known for providing "free" access to information, not all genealogical information on the Internet is "free" of direct cost. Several good commercial suppliers of genealogical information have also emerged on the Web. Estimates of the number of genealogically related Web sites range from 70,000 to more than 100,000. It is very difficult for any one person to keep track of these and to be familiar with them all. Most of these are the Internet equivalent of archives, books, reports, as well as more ephemeral types of information that are analogous to pamphlets or even bubble gum wrappers. In other words something that is just packaging and not directly useful for providing information. Fortunately, the truly useful genealogical research reference tools on the Internet are much fewer in number.

This unit describes ten of the most useful genealogical reference tools on the Internet and the kinds of information found by using them. The ten "best" sites are listed approximately in order of when they would be used in the genealogical research process:

1. Social Security Death Records Index (SSDI) (various Web sites) (Figures 2.1a and 2.1b)
2. Vital Records Information for All States and Territories of the United States & International. www.vitalrec.com/ (Figure 2.2)
3. FamilySearch www.familysearch.org/ (Figure 2.3)
4. American Family Immigration History Center www.ellisislandrecords.org/ (Figure 2.4)
5. RootsWeb Genealogical Data Cooperative www.rootsweb.com (Figure 2.5)
6. USGenWeb Project www.usgenweb.com/ (Figure 2.6)
7. Ancestry.com www.ancestry.com (Figure 2.7)
8. GENDEX - WWW Genealogical Index www.GENDEX.com/GENDEX/ (Figure 2.8)
9. Cyndi's Genealogy Homepage www.CyndisList.com/ (Figure 2.9)
10. NARA National Archives and Records Administration Genealogy Page www.nara.gov/genealogy (Figure 2.10)

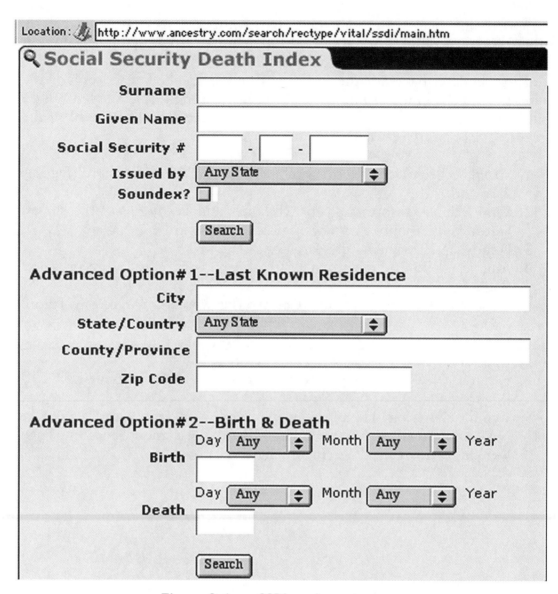

Figure 2.1a.   SSDI on Ancestry.com

These ten sites form a good core genealogical reference e-library collection. They were selected based on my experience over the past several years teaching genealogical research on the Internet and beginning my own family genealogical research.

Alternatively, several Web sites track the most popular genealogical Web sites. Family Chronicle magazine maintains a top 10 "voted best" genealogical Web sites at www.familychronicle.com/webpicks.htm. The Family Chronicle's top 10 genealogical Web sites coincide closely with the selected 10 "best" genealogical reference Web sites discussed in this unit. Genealogy.org

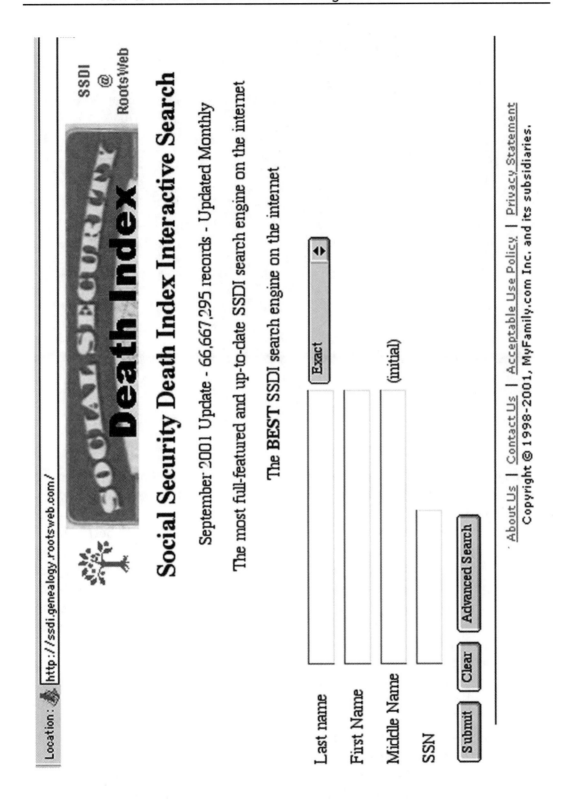

Figure 2.1b.   SSDI Screen from RootsWeb Site

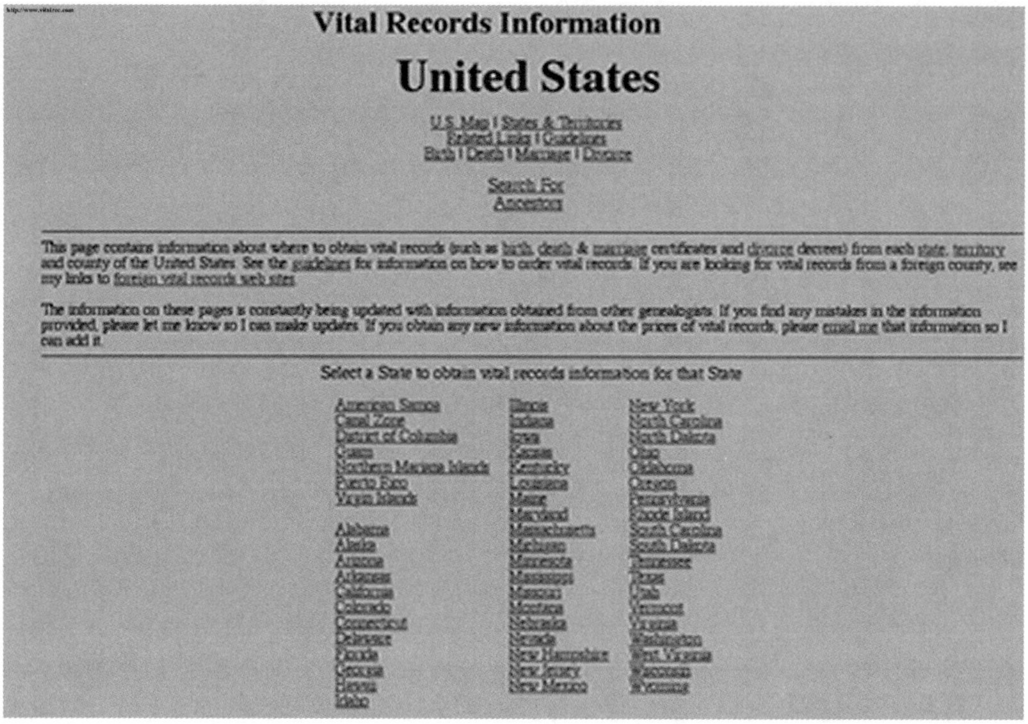

Figure 2.2. Vital Records Information Web Site

(www.genealogy.org/) maintains a weekly hour by hour report of genealogical Web site popularity by number of visits. SurnameWeb (www. surnameweb.com) links to a site that tracks the 100 most popular Web sites by number of visits. Family Tree Magazine selects 101 "voted best" sites at www.familytreemagazine.com/101sites/.

Keep in mind that "most popular" and "best" are not necessarily the same thing. Popularity is measured by the number of times a site is visited or by the number of people who vote for it not necessarily based on the quality of the Web site as a source of genealogical information. Occasionally "popular" sites artificially inflate their visit rate using software that simulates frequent connections or recruit friends, family, employees, or others to vote and vote often. Some of the frequently visited sites are sites offering "free" services for a short time. Many of those are offering services that are already freely available through RootsWeb, USGenWeb or other sites. Some are rehashes of other sites or merely flashy pointers to other sites. Still others are one shot start-ups used to make ad-banner profits. For example, one person puts up or links to the scanned images of marriage records for their state and then puts up lots of ad banners. The ad banners are all over the page (where they are impossible to avoid) and it may be confusing or difficult to get to the actual content. The actual content is frequently available elsewhere such as through RootsWeb or

Figure 2.3.   FamilySearch Web Site

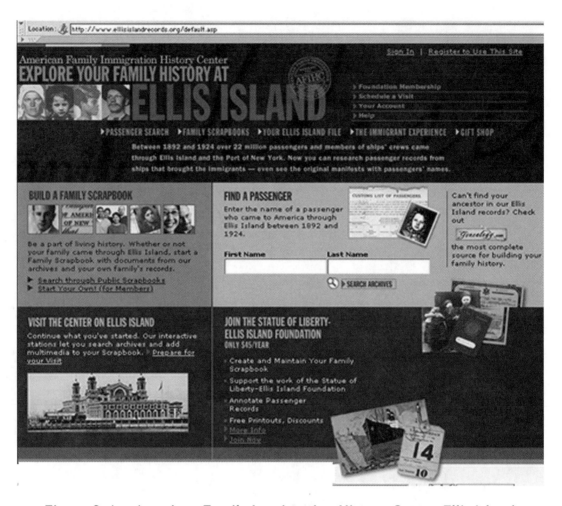

Figure 2.4. American Family Immigration History Center Ellis Island Records Database

a USGenWeb site, with minimal ad banners and a good review process in place. An amazing number of these sites simply link to the originating site, especially in the cases of RootsWeb, USGenWeb, or Ancestry.com databases. In the final analysis, beginning with the best original sources makes more sense than looking for the "popular" sites.

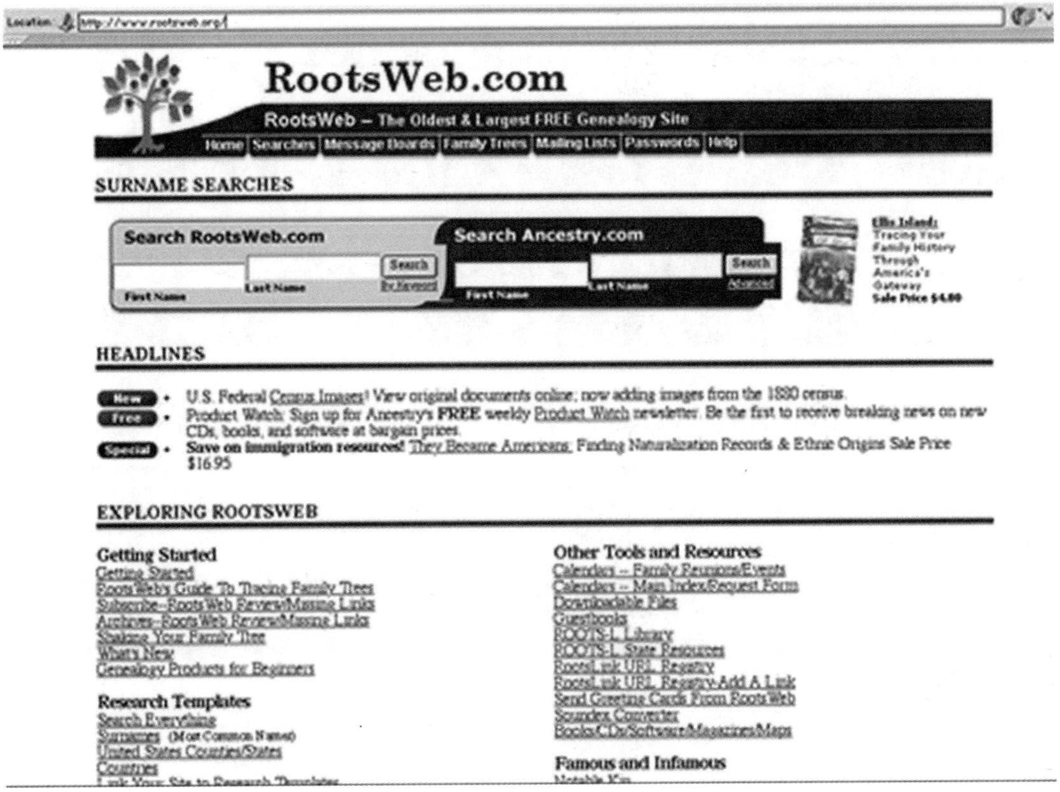

Figure 2.5.   RootsWeb

1. Social Security Death Records (various Web sites)

The Social Security Administration makes available for sale computer file versions of their Death Master File.

"The Social Security Administration (SSA) maintains a Death Master File which is a record of approximately 50 million deaths that were reported to us, in a tape format that is not searchable by the public" (Social Security Administration, 2000).

This file consists of the social security numbers, birth and death dates, and last address known to the Social Security Administration. By using this information, genealogical researchers can order copies of the social security number application forms completed by their deceased family members. Although there are some obvious and not so obvious limitations to this database it is an extremely valuable tool for genealogical researchers.

There are several sites that provide good searchable indexes to the Social Security Death Master File records. Two sites provide advanced search tools and current indexing for current versions: Ancestry.com (www.ancestry.com) and RootsWeb (http://ssdi.rootsweb.com/). Both of these sites allow advanced

Figure 2.6. USGen Web

Social Security Death Index (SSDI) searching, including search by last known residence (city, state, zip code), birth date, death date, as well as by social security number and first and last name.

Successful genealogical research traces lines from the individual to the individual's parents, then grandparents, and so on. The SSDI is used to locate social security information about a specific individual that enables the researcher to order a copy of the individual's social security application form (or related

Figure 2.7. Ancestry.com

filing). The social security application form is very likely to contain information about the parents and place of birth of the individual.

Beginning in 1936, individuals were able to apply for a social security number, to pay into and receive Social Security benefits. When each applicant completed their original Social Security application they answered questions such as their date, city, county, and state of birth; their parents' names, including their mother's birth name; and the applicants' address at the time of the application. These completed records have recently become available for our deceased grandparents and great-grandparents. By using these records, the researcher can document relationships from their grandparents to their parents and so on.

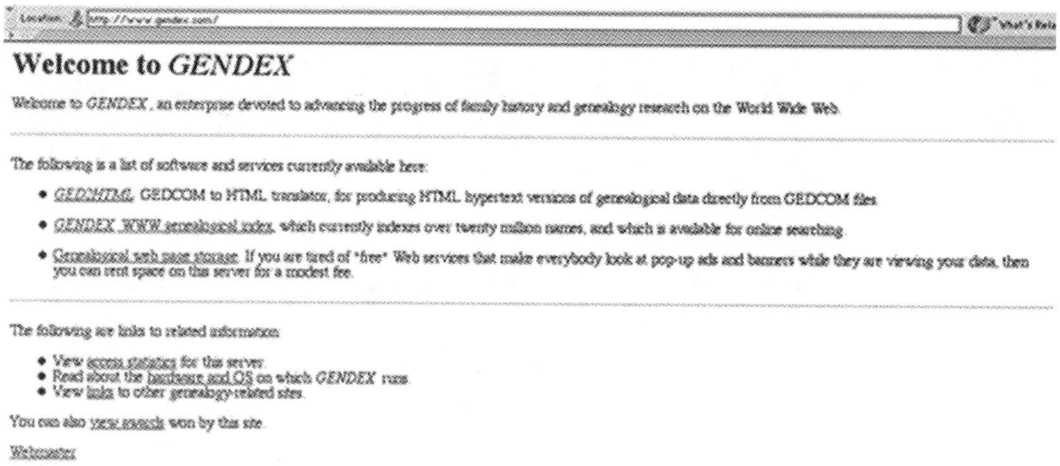

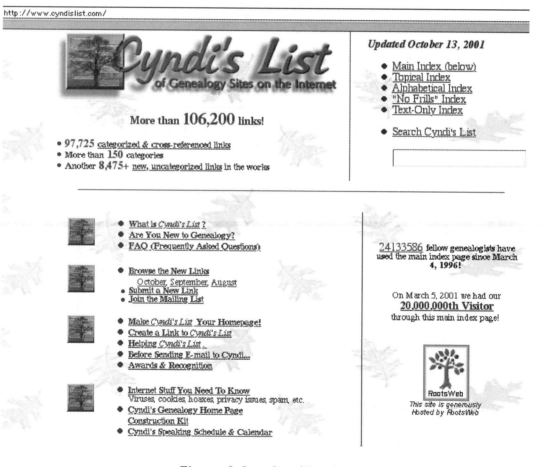

Figure 2.8.   GENDEX

Figure 2.9.   Cyndi's List

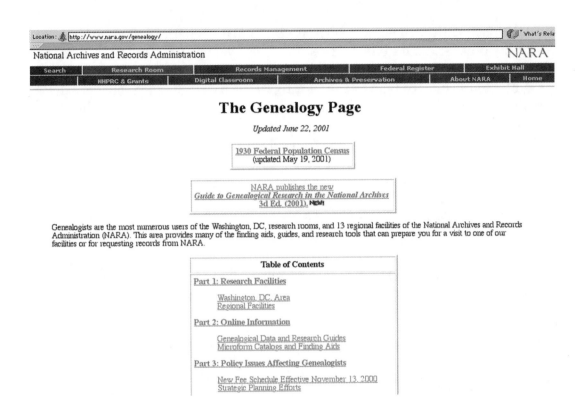

Figure 2.10. **National Archives and Records Administration (NARA) Genealogy Web Page**

For example in researching my own family, starting with my maternal grandmother Alice Jean Finch (Wilson) and my great-grandmother Anna Wilson, I searched the Social Security Death Records index through Ancestry.com's site. Both Ancestry.com and RootsWeb provide a handy form letter to use to order copies of Social Security Application Forms or requests for benefits. The Social Security Application for Alice Finch states that her parents were Anna Schumm and Angier Wilbur Wilson and that she was born in 1910 in Dixon, Illinois in Lee County. Also, from my interview with my mother, I know my great-grandmother's birth name. Ann Wilson's (Schumm) application form was unavailable, so the Social Security Administration sent a copy of her last request for benefits instead. This form states that she was born in 1885 and that her parents were John Schumm and Rosana Whorley and that she was born in Sterling, Illinois, Whiteside County. The index records provide the death date and last address known to the Social Security Administration. With all of this information, I now know where and when to look for and order birth certificates, marriage certificates, death certificates, copies of newspaper stories on these events, etc. and can pursue the next generation of connections into the past. Unfortunately, Angier Wilbur Wilson's name is not in the Index. Since his obituary is dated 1942—only a few years after Social Security began—it is likely he never applied for a Social Security card. However, it is possible that his death was simply not reported to the Social Security Administration in which case they would not include his information in the Death Master File.

My example demonstrates the strengths and limitations of this index as a genealogical research tool. At best, we can only search back two or three generations of our families using the Social Security Death Indexes. Further, records for individuals who died earlier than 1962 are generally not in the Social Security Death Master File. That was the year in which the Social Security Administration began keeping electronic records. The Social Security Administration will be inputting data from records prior to that time. See RootsWeb's Help pages for the SSDI (http://helpdesk.rootsweb.com/help/ssdi.html) for a good basic overview of what is and is not in the database. The Ancestry.com tutorials and articles on the SSDI are also very informative.

2. Vital Records Information for All States and Territories of the United States and International—www.vitalrec.com/

The Vital Records search site is compiled by Elizabeth Orsay. This project began as a volunteer's effort to collect information about how and where to acquire vital statistics information from each state in the United States, as well as other countries. Elizabeth Orsay's project is now funded through ad banners on the Web site. It is well maintained and frequently updated. It is one of the most comprehensive sources of vital records information on the Internet or in any format. It continues to grow in size and complexity.

The main information provided through this Web site concerns which organizations in a given state, county, or country to contact for vital records copies, the policies for providing copies, and guidelines for making requests. Occasionally, vital records may be ordered online or over the telephone from the holding organization.

An increasing number of historical vital records images or transcripts are being made available full-text online and where these are available, the Vital Records Information site provides a link. In 1996, when I first taught genealogical research on the Internet, I said in my lecture that the Internet provided no access to vital records, that is, records of birth, marriage, death, or other vital events. Very soon after that, USGenWeb and other vital records indexing and scanning projects started appearing. This is an area where the information available online increases daily. Elizabeth Orsay monitors those projects and updates the Vital Records Information site as vital records images or transcriptions become available online.

The Vital Records information site compiles and provides information about which states, counties, many provinces, and countries have any of their vital records accessible online or indexed online. In the event that records are not available or indexed online, this site provides postal mail or telephone ordering information.

An important aspect to be aware of when using this site is that it is organized state by state, county by county, province by province, country by country. The best strategy in using the information through this Web site is to take advantage of that organization and click through to the vital records offices Web sites to find out what is actually available online or through their offices. Some records offices, in some states, for some counties provide searchable indexes of some of the available records. In some cases, the records available for searching or ordering are limited to certain date ranges and regions. For example, in Illinois, the Illinois Statewide Marriage Index (www. cyberdriveillinois.com/departments/Archives/marriage.html) allows searching of marriage records for many counties between the dates 1763–1900. With this information the researcher can order copies of the original records from the holding archives. In Ohio, the Death Certificates Index (www. ohiohistory.org/dindex/) searches an index of death certificates from 1913-1937 for most counties in Ohio. Records can then be ordered from the Ohio Historical Society archives. If records are available for in-person viewing and/ or copying at local archives and libraries that information will be noted. Some states and counties participate in a commercial service called "VitalCheck" (www.vitalcheck.com) that expedites on-line or telephone ordering of vital records. Researchers could also connect directly to the VitalCheck Web site, but it saves time to read through what each state or county actually has available before doing that.

For example, the Vital Records search site information for Medina County Ohio includes a link to that state's Online Death Certificate Index, 1913-1937 created by the Ohio Historical Society (www.ohiohistory.org/dindex/ search.cfm). The site also includes mailing and other contact information for the Ohio Historical Society, as well as links to the Ohio Historical Society Web site where information about what records for which counties are available for which time periods.

There are full-text transcribed or scanned images of vital records including census data online, but only for some very limited date ranges and subject areas. Some of these are part of the USGenWeb project. Commercial genealogical data providers have also begun to provide full-text transcribed or scanned images of actual vital records through their Web sites.

3. FamilySearch—www.familysearch.org/

The FamilySearch Web site provided by the Church of Jesus Christ of Latter Day Saints (LDS) is extraordinary!

The LDS church believes that one should identify one's ancestors as part of

---

Success Story 2.1 Using Genealogical Reference Tools on the Web by Mining Online Information

Sandra Yorkell-Parker syparker@nidlink.com (Bonner County Wyoming Genealogical Society President & USGenWeb Coordinator)

I enjoy the Familysearch.org site. It has been very helpful in my research. I recently found more of my husband's family there and was very happy. Have more of his cousins to write to and exchange information now. The surname mailing lists are great as well because at times they will get you in touch with others who are researching the same names or who know someone who is working on them. Recently while using a surname list I was contacted by a relative who had the information I was seeking on a great aunt of mine on my father's side of the family. Needless to say I now have up to the 1920s I believe of family and haven't had an opportunity to get to see if there are others of that line who are researching the family. The Internet has been a boon for me and I am on numerous mailing lists that have to do with my heritage. I also send on addresses of sites to people who are researching those areas as well.

Using the Canada411 site has also helped me as I am of Canadian descent and was looking for any living cousins. I was very successful in this as I found a number of them and now have their history included with mine to make a larger book for us.

Genealogy on the Internet is fun and can be very helpful when you know where to look and how to look.

---

one's religious obligations. The FamilySearch Web site provides more details on this belief of the LDS church.

In pursuing this religious obligation, the LDS church and its members have kept incredible detailed records and have archived large quantities of copies of vital records and documentation. Many of the microformed records are available at local family history centers. The FamilySearch.org site has location and contact information for the various local family history locations throughout the world. A searchable index to much of the collection, and to some full-text records (Family Group Sheets) are available through the FamilySearch Web site. The Web site also provides information on ordering copies of the microformed documentation from the LDS Family History Library in Salt Lake City, Utah.

"The number of U.S. county clerk's offices, registries of probate and deeds, foreign parishes, and other jurisdictional record holders that have had their records microfilmed by the LDS church is staggering to contemplate" (Stratton, 1988:8).

The FamilySearch Web site indexes data from the LDS Church Ancestral File collection, as well as the International Genealogy Index (IGI). These collections were first begun back in 1894. The publication of the indexes to these publications is an enormous contribution to genealogical research. The Ancestral File is a collection of "over 35 million names linked into family groups and pedigrees." The Ancestral File database indexes "Family Group Sheets" contributed by individual members of the LDS Church. The Ancestral File database includes dates and places of births, marriages, and deaths as known, documented, or surmised by the data contributors. In order to obtain documentation for information found in the Ancestral file, it is necessary to contact the individuals who contributed the information. The contributor's name and contact information is provided in the database.

"Ancestral File is a collection of genealogical information taken from Pedigree Charts and Family Group Records submitted to the Family History Department since 1978. The information has not been verified against any official records. Since the information in Ancestral File is contributed, it is the responsibility of those who use the file to verify its accuracy" (FamilySearch, 2001).

The IGI, in contrast, is a project to index and make searchable a collection of birth and marriage information extracted from civil and church records from all over the world, by the LDS church.

"Secondary source information at the library ranges from the scholarly to the routine. The International Genealogical Index (IGI) is one of the more useful secondary sources, though its limitations should be understood. Volunteers transcribe vital records obtained from all over the world, and these are computerized and put on microfiche. Information is sequenced by geographic area—by state for the United States—and then by name in alphabetical order. Birth information gives the person's name, date and place of birth, and parents' names, while marriage information appears under both the bride's and groom's names, together with date and place of marriage, and spouse's name. Death records are not contained in the IGI . . . " (Stratton, 1988:8).

While most of the data indexed in the IGI is from primary records, some is from what the LDS calls "family group sheets." This is data provided by individuals that may or may not be supported by documentation from primary records or by contemporary accounts.

For example, data in the FamilySearch.org database on the individual named "Albert Engelbrecht birth Abt. 1877 <Belvidere, Boone, Illinois>" is from details submitted in a family group record. The submitter's name and address is linked from the record. It would be necessary to contact the submitter to obtain documentation regarding the individual "Albert Engelbrecht." However, information provided in the FamilySearch.org database for the individual named "Gilbert M. FINCH Birth: 11 Mar 1867 Of, Greenwich, Frfld, Connecticut" is documented by fiche number 1553744 in the IGI records. A copy of that document can be ordered on microfilm from any LDS Church Family History Center or by visiting the Family History Library in Salt Lake City, Utah. The IGI search results and most of the Ancestral File results can be downloaded directly to the researcher's computer as Gedcom files.

The FamilySearch search tool can limit a search to only the IGI records, or to only the Ancestral File records as preferred.

The FamilySearch.org site also provides extensive research guidance on topics from beginning research to finding and working with data in censuses, immigration records, international research and more.

4. American Family Immigration History Center— www.ellisislandrecords.org/

The American Family Immigration History Center's Ellis Island passenger records database (www.ellisislandrecords.org/) went online on April 16, 2001. The American Family Immigration History Center's Ellis Island passenger records database is:

"... the painstaking work performed by thousands of volunteers from The Church of Jesus Christ of Latter-day Saints. Their efforts helped produce the computerized Ellis Island passenger records database recently contributed by the Church to the National Park Service, for use by The Statue of Liberty— Ellis Island Foundation, Inc. The Ellis Island database provides easy access to the passenger arrival records of approximately 22 million individuals whose names appear in the original ships' passenger manifests for the Port of New York from 1892 to 1924" (American Family Immigration History Center, 2001). The project was funded by donations to the Ellis Island Foundation, Inc.

The database may be searched without registering, but in order to view the full passenger record registration is required. Registration is free, but researchers are invited to become members of the Ellis Island Foundation, Inc. and make appropriate contributions.

The Ellis Island Records database includes arrival records with passenger information based on original passenger lists (known as "manifests"), text versions of the manifests, and some ship pictures. It is important to be aware of the dates between which records are available and also that this database contains only Ellis Island arrivals. Many immigrants arrived in the United States prior to 1892 and after 1924. Many came either across the Mexican or Canadian borders or through California. These entries were not generally recorded. These topics will be discussed when we look at the National Archives and Records Administration Genealogy (www.nara.gov/genealogy) page below and in Part 3.

"The companies that transported immigrant passengers kept detailed passenger lists, called 'ship manifests.' Manifests were filled out not at Ellis Island but at the immigrants' ports of departure. Passengers were asked a series of questions; their answers were entered in the manifests. Ellis Island inspectors then used the manifests to examine immigrants" (Ellis Island Records, 2001).

On some passenger records, the researcher can read annotations regarding passengers supplied by members of the Ellis Island Foundation. Foundation members may add annotations based on the information they have about a given passenger.

In order to use this database effectively, researchers must know the names and possible variants of the names of their ancestors. It is helpful for the researcher to know the place their immigrant ancestor came from or the place of residence declared, their ethnicity, their approximate age when they arrived, and the approximate date when they arrived in the United States. The passenger's port of departure or the name of the ship also can be used to narrow a search to a specific individual if this information is known. These searches can be very challenging. For example, I searched for my husband's grandmother using this tool. The actual "1954 Address Report Card" form that Helen Churpek (Kovacs) (Solomon) filed with the INS on January 29, 1954 states that she entered the United States at Ellis Island on December 17, 1905. She was born in Hungary, so her ethnicity is probably Magyar or possibly Hebrew given her birth name. Hungary, especially prior to World War I, was a multi-ethnic society. Helen's birth year is given as 1880, which would make her 24-25 when she arrived in the United States. The INS form states that either she reported in 1953 using the name Helen Kovacs or was originally registered as a resident alien under that name. Interviews with living contemporaries of Helen state that her father's name was "Louse" (possibly Lajos, Laos, Laszlo, Louis, or Lewis) Solomon and her mother was Mary Komaromi (of the village of Komarom?) and that the family came from Ublya, Hungary. We do not know if Helen traveled with her birth family or with her husband. Using Google, www.google.com, to search for "Ublya," we located an 1882 gazetteer of Hungary at the Radix Hungarian Genealogy site www.bogardi.com/gen/. We found that Ublya was in the Zemplen megye (county) and in the Szinnai jàràs (district). This gazetteer provides a listing for all of the villages in that and other districts of Zemplen megye. We used this list to check for Ublya or likely alternative villages listed in the passenger records search results as places of origin.

A search of the Ellis Island Records Database retrieves no record for a Helen with any of the known names for her. Using possible Hungarian versions of the name Helen: Helena, Ilona, Elana, and the long stretch Jlona, the search also failed to retrieve a record within the date range 1904–1907. The next step was to try to locate Louse Solomon (also Salamon, Soloman, and other variant spellings). The database allows searching by the first letter of the name, so we searched for "L Solomon." We also searched for common Hungarian variants on Solomon, such as Salamon and Saloman. There again the search failed to locate a likely passenger. We know from Helen's son Joseph Kovacs's B&O Railroad Pension form copy—obtained from the Social Security Administration after search of the SSDI—that Helen's first husband's name was John Kovacs. A search of the Ellis Island Records database on the name Kovacs with variants, limited to Magyar ethnicity and to the year 1905, returns more than 900 passengers. According to the article "Hungarian Names 101" by Walraven van Nijmegen at www.geocities.com/Athens/1336/magyarnames101. html, Kovacs is Hungarian for Smith and apparently is just as common a name. We searched for John Kovacs arriving 1904-1907 and being at least the same age as or older than Helen, that is 23-60. No records for John Kovacs fit the times, residences, and other information that we know. The next step is to try some possible versions of the name John: Janos, Johannes, Jovan, also Jòszef. Jòszef was suggested by the same living family member who provided Helen's father's name. None of the Jovans or Jòszefs fit our criteria. There were no Johannes Kovacs listed in our date range. The name Janos Kovacs retrieved several hundred individuals arriving during that time and of approximately the appropriate age. We narrowed the search down to just 1905. This narrowed down the search to 90 passenger records. We began scanning for places of residence in Zemplen megye, Hungary. At this writing we are still slowly checking each passenger record and ship's manifest to try to locate a Janos that might come from the area of Zemplen megye, is married, and perhaps accompanied by a wife that might be Helen. It increases our challenge that historically, between 1899 and 1913, more than 10,000 Hungarians came to the United States. Many of these came from Zemplen megye (northern Hungary prior to World War I, now mostly a part of the Slovak Republic).

5. RootsWeb Genealogical Data Cooperative— www.rootsweb.com

RootsWeb is the oldest and most comprehensive genealogy reference Web site. It is a classic metasite. RootsWeb is both browseable by project or topic area, as well as searchable. The RootsWeb site is absolutely essential for doing your own or helping others with their genealogical research since most of the other good genealogical sites on the Web are linked from the RootsWeb main or subsidiary pages. RootsWeb provides a central meeting and communications center for genealogical researchers worldwide, as well. In Part 3, RootsWeb's directory of genealogical discussion lists and genealogical Web boards will be center stage. RootsWeb also provides some of the best online genealogical research tutorials and articles, for beginners through advanced researchers.

The first screen of the main RootsWeb page offers the options to search the RootsWeb Web site and meta-search-engine for surnames, the Genseeker database of family history and genealogy homepages, the Social Security Death Records database, and the WorldConnect database of genealogical data (GEDCOM) files on the Web. Paging down the main RootsWeb page shows a classified directory of RootsWeb-sponsored efforts to publish genealogy information and links to other related project Web pages.

The RootsWeb volunteer organization sponsors the lion's share of important and useful genealogical projects on the Web including:

- USGenWeb Project—"The USGenWeb Project consists of a group of volunteers working together to provide Internet Web sites for genealogical research in every county and every state of the United States. The project is non-commercial and fully committed to free access for everyone" (USGenWeb, 2001).
- WorldGenWeb projects—International genealogical research volunteers maintain many Web sites for regional and country specific genealogical research support. The WorldGenWeb project compiles and links to those sites and helps to coordinate them (http://worldgenweb.org/).
- FreeBMD (England and Wales)—"FreeBMD stands for Free Births, Marriages, and Deaths. The FreeBMD Project's objective is to provide free Internet access to the Civil Registration index information for England and Wales. The Civil Registration system for recording births, marriages, and deaths in England and Wales has been in place since 1837 and is one of the most significant single resources for genealogical research back to Victorian times" (FreeBMD, 2001).
- FreeReg (UK)—This is a volunteer project to "provide free Internet searches of baptism, marriage, and burial records, which have been transcribed from parish and non-conformist church registers in the UK" (FreeReg, 2001).
- Genealogy.org—Genealogy Web site registration and search tool, Gensite, a genealogy events listing, as well as the WorldConnect GEDCOM tools site (http://wc.rootsweb.com/wchistory.html).
- Immigrant Ships Transcribers Guild—Volunteer project to decipher and transcribe passenger lists, then publishes them on the Web.
- Obituary Daily Times—Volunteer project to index obituaries in local newspapers.
- Random Acts of Genealogical Kindness—Group of volunteers who are willing to look up specific facts in certain genealogical records. Volunteers will do one lookup per month.
- Cyndi's List—One of the most comprehensive genealogical metasites.

This is a selective list of some of the more important projects sponsored and hosted by RootsWeb.

At this writing, RootsWeb is now sponsored by Ancestry.com, but it is still "The Internet's Oldest and Largest FREE Genealogy Site." The core RootsWeb group is a community of volunteer genealogical researchers who with financial support from Myfamily.com—Ancestry.com's parent company—will continue to provide access to:

> "19,000 mailing lists, the hundreds of millions of names in free genealogy databases, the interactive learning guides, the weekly RootsWeb Review and Missing Links, the numerous tools for tracing your family history, the tens of thousands of message boards, the thousands of independently authored web sites. RootsWeb will still support worthy genealogy projects and societies, such as the USGenWeb Project (www.USGenWeb.org), the Immigrant Ships Transcribers Guild (ISTG.rootsweb.com) and the FreeBMD Project (FreeBMD.rootsweb.com), and other groups that provide free genealogical resources" (RootsWeb, 2001).

Activity 2.4 walks you through searching the resources available through RootsWeb Cooperative's global search tool. RootsWeb resources will appear several times in subsequent parts as well.

6. USGenWeb Project—www.usgenweb.com/

USGenWeb is the source of a large number of the most useful primary genealogical documents that are being published on the Web. USGenWeb is also hosted and sponsored by the RootsWeb Cooperative. It is a tremendous organization of volunteers who work to publish primary genealogical data for a particular locality, in particular counties in a given state. There is a tremendous range of data available depending on which county and state project is viewed.

USGenWeb volunteers have scanned and transcribed hundreds of census records, local vital records, newspaper accounts, gravestone inscriptions, and more. The one difficulty in using this reference tool is that the available information varies considerably between the county projects. Where one county has numerous projects and very active volunteers, another may have very few projects and fewer active volunteers. For example, the Lee County Illinois USGenweb (www.rootsweb.com/~illee/index.htm) seems to have a number of active volunteers. The Lee County Illinois volunteers have transcribed many useful files and created surname indexes for Lee County histories and newspapers. In one source, "Surname index of the Amboy News Paper from July 1882 to Jan 1886" compiled by Bob Boward, I found five mentions of my maternal great-grandfather Gilbert P. Finch. I e-mailed a request for copies of those stories and was able to provide the page number and column of each mention, as well as the date of the newspaper. The fees for the Lee County Genealogical Society volunteers' research services and copying charges are clearly detailed on their Web site. Also, in the Lee County Illinois USGenWeb archives, I found a complete transcription of a Sept. 18-21, 1918 *Dixon Evening Telegraph* story listing all of the men 18-45 who had signed up for military service along with their serial numbers. This listing included my maternal great-grandfather Angier Wilson's name and serial number. WWI ended November 11, 1918 and my great-grandfather was not drafted.

The USGenWeb Project Archives, also known as the USGenWeb Digital Library, is supported by hundreds of volunteers who transcribe public domain records including census, land, marriage, birth, death, cemetery records, and tombstone transcriptions. The USGenWeb Digital Library is searchable by keyword and also browseable by state (http://searches.rootsweb.com/htdig/search.html).

The USGenWeb Digital Library includes:

- Census Project and Census Images—Volunteers indexing, transcribing, and scanning census images for their counties and states.
- Digital Map Library Project—Volunteers scanning historical and current maps for use by genealogical researchers.
- Obituary Project—Volunteers transcribing obituaries and sharing them online.
- Pension Project—Volunteers indexing, transcribing, and scanning pension records from the U.S. wars prior to 1900.
- Tombstone Project—Volunteers traveling to cemeteries and transcribing and sharing tombstone data online.
- Church Project—Volunteers indexing, transcribing, and scanning church records.
- Marriage Project—Volunteers transcribing marriage records and sharing them online.
- Special Collections Project—Volunteers indexing, transcribing, or scanning all kinds of miscellaneous materials that cross county, state, or international boundaries in scope.
- Lineage Project—Site where each researcher can track and share information on their descent from any particular ancestor born before December 31, 1850 and who must have lived in the U.S. at some time.
- The Kidz Project—materials and resources to assist children in doing their own genealogy research.

Activity 2.5 guides you through checking what kinds of primary data, if any, have been published for a state and county of your choice.

7. Ancestry.com—www.ancestry.com

The commercial genealogy publisher Ancestry.com provides online searchable access to hundreds of genealogical indexes, publications, and miscellaneous databases. Scanned images of census and other records are also available through the Ancestry.com Web site. Ancestry.com is a subscription service, but they provide free access to databases such as the Social Security Death Records, and frequently offer one or more of their subscription databases for free trial searching during any given month. There are more than 3,000 individual databases indexed by Ancestry.com. They also provide tutorials and a newsletter with articles by professional genealogical researchers on topics important to genealogical researchers using the Internet. Their subscription fee is very reasonable and they do negotiate with libraries to provide library subscriptions for patron access. In partnership with the Gale Group, Ancestry.com publishes AncestryPlus, an enhanced version of Ancestry.com for libraries. Connect to the Gale Group Web site (www.galegroup.com) for more information about AncestryPlus access.

The Ancestry.com databases include indexes to primary resources such as vital records, but they may also be based on secondary resources. It is advisable to click on the Extended Description link provided for each database to learn more about what is actually being searched. Ancestry.com's main search tool searches all of their indexed databases from the home page. However, it is also possible to search in individual databases one at a time.

For example the Hope, Ontario 1880 Census is an index to the actual Ontario census record. However, the database titled "Nash County, North Carolina Vital Records Abstracts" is a transcription from an undocumented genealogy narrative of questionable origin. This database was discussed extensively during January 2001 on the discussion list Genealib: Librarians Serving Genealogists (www.cas.usf.edu/lis/genealib/). Specifically:

The database provider, Cynthia Herrin, describes the source book as follows:

"In 1909, a local genealogical group published a series of county histories for northeast North Carolina. Families of Early North Carolina is separated into three sections. The first section is a narrative describing the people and adventures of the county. This part was enjoyable and gossipy, although I am suspicious of the accuracy of some of the birth and marriage dates provided. The authors may have guessed. However, it was rich with family connections and with personal stories, many of them not complimentary to those involved. I briefly included bits that would provide interest (murders, suspected murders, family feuding, illnesses and drunkenness, etc), hoping to tip researchers off to the existence of other family records that might be found in court proceedings or newspapers . . . " (Ancestry.com, 2001).

Recently Ancestry.com began adding image databases, including census and

Civil War records, to their subscription services. These are currently browseable, but not searchable. This is a work in progress. These images are of fairly high quality, but difficult to manipulate without the MrSID graphics viewer browser plugin from LizardTech (www.lizardtech.com). This is a very simple but powerful graphics viewing tool. As of this writing the Ancestry.com site doesn't provide the standard MrSID files required to use the Macintosh OS version of the MrSID plugin. Figures 1.6 and 1.7 in Part 1 were extracted from Census Images downloaded from Ancestry.com. Browsing through pages and pages of U.S. Federal Census is very time consuming. By accessing these images online, the researcher saves travel time, and won't have to leave when the library or archives closes. However, if the original records were badly preserved, damaged, microfilmed badly, incorrect, or any number of other problems the online images only reflect the state of the original records.

8. GENDEX—WWW Genealogical Index—(www.GENDEX.com/GENDEX/)

GENDEX is an independent searchable database of family history Web pages and GEDCOM files. This database contains basic genealogically-related information on more than 20 million names. This is a truly "free" place to publish family history Web pages. The site also has a software tool for converting GEDCOM files—produced from almost any decent genealogical database software—directly HTML for publishing on the Web. It is maintained by Gene Stark (www.GENDEX.com/GENDEX/mailto.html).

There are two levels of search access for GENDEX: registered and unregistered. If the researcher registers and pays a small fee, the search engine allows greater sorting and filtering of each search. Another feature of GENDEX search tool is that the researcher can also search by Soundex names.

"The Soundex is a coded last name (surname) index based on the way a name sounds rather than the way it is spelled. Surnames that sound the same, but are spelled differently, like SMITH and SMYTH, have the same code and are filed together. The Soundex coding system was developed so that you can find a surname even though it may have been recorded under various spellings" (National Archives and Records Administration, 2001).

GENDEX was one of the first projects to collect and index family history Web pages into a searchable index. The display is extremely simple and is based on HTML files converted from GEDCOM files published on Web pages. Each search result is sorted first by surname and then alphabetically by given name and then by alphabetic ranges of given names. The listed individual links connect to the original Web site where the information is published. The letter (i) denotes a link with information about who published the genealogical information and how to contact them.

As you can tell by the number of sites indexed by GENDEX and some of the other metasites, family history Web pages are the most numerous individual type of genealogical site on the Internet.

There are many family history Web sites that are well done and documented. Some information provided, though, is inaccurate, some information is deliberately made up, and still other information is wishful thinking. In Part 3, we'll talk more about this kind of sharing of genealogical data.

Activity 2.7 steps you through using GENDEX to locate specific genealogical data for a family name of your choice.

9. Cyndi's Genealogy Homepage—www.CyndisList.com/

Cyndi's List (www.CyndisList.com/) is compiled by genealogical researcher Cyndi Howells. It is the favorite site of many genealogical researchers. In fact almost all other metasites link back to Cyndi's List. At this writing Cyndi's List is:

"5 Years Old - March 4, 2001 More than 90,300 links! 81,550 links, categorized & cross-referenced, in over 140 categories Another 8,700+ uncategorized new links in the works" (Cyndi's List, 2001).

This collection is the most comprehensive electronic library of genealogical Web sites available. Between them, Cyndi's List and RootsWeb encompass most of the genealogical resources on the Web and are almost always linked from the other metasites. Cyndi's List is very well-organized by subject classification, then by general genealogical category, and then by ethnic and country origins. Just about every area of genealogical research is covered. One particularly valuable aspect of Cyndi's List is the inclusion of the lists of genealogical journals that are online or at least have Web sites. The coverage of international, African American, and Native American genealogical resources is marvelous.

Cyndi's List is browseable and searchable. The researcher may connect from the table of contents to the category listing, topical, or alphabetical index. It is rewarding to browse Cyndi's List by choosing a subject area and clicking the hierarchical links to get to pages of links to specific Web sites. There are other directories and metasites and some of these are included in the "Other Useful Genealogical Reference Sites" section of this part.

Activity 2.4 introduces Cyndi's List and lets you compare it to other genealogical metasites. You will encounter this marvelous metasite again in future parts as well.

10. NARA National Archives and Records Administration Genealogy Page—www.nara.gov/genealogy

This site is an essential tool for genealogical researchers. It provides extensive information about the kinds of records held by the United States National Archives and Records Administration, as well as instructions for ordering copies of records or purchasing microfilmed records. The NARA Web site explains what information is contained in military records, U.S. Federal Census data, immigration and naturalization records, census enumeration district maps, as well as how to obtain these records.

We'll revisit this site again in Part 3 with more discussion of how to use the NARA Web site to locate and obtain documentation of genealogical data.

Other Useful Genealogical Reference Sites

The Lineages, Inc. (www.lineages.com) provides "Research Rooms" for genealogical research guidance and links to some valuable information sites. The "American Research Room" lists archives and libraries with online or physical collections, courthouses, and other sites. Lineages, Inc. also sponsors the JewishGen.org Web site. We'll look at this again briefly in Part 4. The Lineages.com site also links to an extensive U.S. Gazetteer for use in identifying place names. Gazetteers can help identify place names mentioned when the researcher interviews living family members.

The U.S. Census Bureau (www.census.gov/cgi-bin/gazetteer) maintains an excellent online gazetteer for the U.S. Listings contain population information, place type, location, enumeration district, and more for each place listed.

For example, my husband's grandfather kept saying that for the 1920 U.S. Federal Census his father, Istvan "Steve" Kacsandy, and the family were living in "Smitten" Pennsylvania near Pittsburgh. He was quite firm on this place and his pronunciation of the place name. A scan through the gazetteer's listings of place names in Pennsylvania that begin with "sm" shows no "Smitten" but does locate "Smithton" as a borough in Westmoreland County, Pennsylvania. The Tiger map provided through the gazetteer site doesn't help us to locate the proximity of Smithton to Pittsburgh. Using the USGenweb site for Pennsylvania (www.pa-roots.com/~pagenweb/) we located a map of Pennsylvania counties showing that Westmoreland County is just south and east of Pittsburgh. The Istvan "Steve" Kacsandy family was located in the 1920 Census images in the enumeration district 213 in Westmoreland County: "Scottdale borough.;South Huntingdon township (part of), excluding Smithton and West Newton boroughs. Nixon and South Huntingdon districts." We showed the record to Grandpa who said "Yes! That's it! 'Smitten' near Pittsburgh." The gazetteer and other maps on the Web aided us to locate the census record for the family.

SurnameWeb (www.surnameweb.org/) was founded by Dennis Partridge (partridge@knology.net) in May 1997. SurnameWeb is maintained by the SurnameWeb team. Current and former team members and their responsibilities and qualifications are listed at www.surnameweb.org/team.htm.

On January 6, 2001, SurnameWeb claimed to index: "116,631 surnames 3,152 Surname Resource Centers 80,069 web page listings 10,492 origin listings! 5,723 Researcher Listings" (SurnameWeb, 2001).

If by some chance you can't find a surname you are looking for by using the SurnameWeb search tool, they offer an option for an expanded Web search. AccessGenealogy (www.accessgenealogy.com/) is SurnameWeb's "sister site." This site has collected scanned images of genealogical books and is making them available free on the Web as the "Free Online Genealogy Library." These are identified by images of their title pages and the contact information for the persons responsible for scanning the texts. AccessGenealogy is also organizing indexes to census and other records specific to Native American genealogical research, as well as military records.

Activity 2.4 provides an opportunity to evaluate SurnameWeb and compare it with other genealogical metasites.

Obituary Central (www.obitcentral.com/) is a metasite focused on sources of obituaries or obituary location tools. Obituaries are an excellent source of leads in genealogical research.

Sometimes individuals may be expecting that census records will contain detailed information about their ancestors. Census records are counts of people, occupations, economic factors, and various other details, but they are not vital records in terms of documentation of birth/death/marriage/origins, although some of that type of information may be incidentally in some records.

UMI's subscription database "Genealogy & Local History Online" (http://genealogy.umi.com/) contains a growing collection of searchable images of genealogy and local history serials, books, and primary documents.

The United States Historical Census Data Browser at the University of Virginia Library site (http://fisher.lib.virginia.edu/census/) may be helpful in learning exactly what details were surveyed in a given census year. The United States Historical Census Data Browser explains in detail what information was gathered in each census and lets you extract summary/group data and statistics.

The Web-published article "Finding Treasures in the U.S. Census" by Judy Hanna (www.firstct.com/fv/uscensus.html) explains how to derive real genealogical and other information from the census data.

Donovan Ackley maintains the Ohio Public Library Information Network (OPLIN) Genealogical Resources collection (http://oplin.lib.oh.us). Although the site is Ohio-centric, Donovan has collected and annotated an unparalleled collection of genealogical software, genealogical information sources, and more.

Each month he publishes a short article focusing on some helpful tip for doing genealogical research in general and on the Internet in particular.

Helm's Genealogy Toolbox (www.genealogytoolbox.com/) is an excellent collection of genealogical Web sites. Matt Helm maintains this collection and organizes it clearly. This Web site is also home to the Journal of Online Genealogy (www.onlinegenealogy.com), a monthly e-journal dedicated to genealogical research on the Internet.

Last but not least, the general Web search tools Google (www.google.com) and Altavista (www.altavista.com) are particularly useful for finding genealogy Web pages. Google is uncannily effective for retrieving just the right Web page. For example, the Hungarian Names 101 site mentioned above was located using Google and the search "Hungarian Names." Altavista is invaluable because of its advanced search features and the huge size of its database of Web pages. The Internet Public Library (www.ipl.org) and Librarian's Index to the Internet (www.lii.org) are two good Web directories for identifying quality genealogical Web sites.

There are thousands of genealogical information sites on the Internet. Some few of these are high-quality sources of genealogical research information. The sites discussed in this unit are the best places to begin genealogical research on the Internet. The best way to learn about the best Web sites for genealogical reference is to connect and learn about them directly. The activities that follow are designed for guided discovery learning of the best genealogical reference sites. The activities are available on the companion Web site (see the Introduction to the Book and Companion Web site).

References

American Family Immigration History Center. 2001. [Online]. Available: www.ellisislandrecords.org [2001, October 22].

Ancestry.com. 2001. [Online]. Available: www.ancestry.com/search/rectype/inddbs/4682.htm [2001, October 23].

Cyndi's List. 1996. [Online]. Available: www.cyndislist.com [2001, March 4].

Ellis Island Records. 2001. [Online]. Available: www.ellisislandrecords.org [2001, October 22].

Family Search. 2001. [Online]. Available: www.familysearch.org [2001, October 22].

FreeBMD. 2001. [Online]. Available: http://freebmd.rootsweb.com/ [2001, October 23].

FreeReg. 2001. [Online]. Available: http://freereg.rootsweb.com/ [2001, October 23].

National Archives and Records Administration. 2001. [Online]. Available: www.nara.gov/genealogy/soundex/soundex.html [2001, October 23].

Renick, Barbara, and Richard S. Wilson. 1999. *The Internet for Genealogists: A Beginners's Guide*, Fourth Edition. La Habra, Calif.: Compuology.

RootsWeb. 2001. [Online]. Available: http://rootsweb.com/rootsweb.com/ [2001, October 23].

Social Security Administration. 2000. [Online]. Available: www.ssa.gov/pubs/ [2001, May 5].

Stratton, E.A. 1988. *Applied Genealogy*. Salt Lake City, Utah: Ancestory Inc.

SurnameWeb. 2001. [Online]. Available: www.surnameweb.org [2001, January 6].

USGenWeb Project. 2001. [Online]. Available: www.usgenweb.org/about/about.html [2001, October 23].

Activity 2.1. Identifying Recent Ancestors in the Social Security Death Master File Indexes at Ancestry.Com and RootsWeb

Overview:

In this activity you will compare the Social Security Death Index search tools at Ancestry.com and RootsWeb.

STEP 1.   Connect to **Ancestry.com** *http://www.ancestry.com*. Click on the link for "Social Security Death Index"

STEP 2.   Read completely through this page. Click on the link for "Frequently Asked Questions" and read through these questions and the answers. Return to the "Social Security Death Index" search page.

STEP 3.   Search on the "Given" name Gilbert surname Finch, use the "Last known residence" Illinois. How many results do you find? What is the birthdate and year of the Gilbert Finch who was last known to reside in Dixon, Illinois?

STEP 4.   Search on a name and last known residence of your choice. Did you have any results?

❑ Yes   ❑ No

How many?

Do you know if this individual is a member of your family?

❑ Yes   ❑ No

What evidence do you have or see that demonstrates that the individual record you see is for a member of your family? What is the relationship to you?

STEP 5.   Connect to the **RootsWeb** site at *http://www.rootsweb.com*. Click on the "Searches" tab/button. Then click on the link for "Social Security Death Index."

STEP 6.   Read completely through this page. Click on the link "For more info about the SSDI" read through this article. Return to the "Social Security Death Index" search page. Click on the "Advanced Search" button.

STEP 7.   Search on the first name Gilbert last name Finch, use the "Last residence" Illinois (IL). How many results do you find? Are they the same results as you got in searching on this name in the Ancestry.com version of the Social Security Death Index?

STEP 8.   Search on the same name and last known residence as you searched in STEP 4. Did you have the same results in this search as you had in searching Ancestry.com?

❏ Yes   ❏ No

If your results were not the same in searching the RootsWeb Social Security Death Index as in searching the Ancestry.com Social Security Death Index, how were the results different?

Note: If you are working self-paced and would like instructor feedback e-mail your responses and questions to *diane@kovacs.com*

Activity 2.2.   Locating Vital Records Information for All States and Territories of the United States, Canada, and Other International

Overview:

In this activity you will search for vital records and statistics sites for your state. Using Elizabeth Orsay's directory of vital statistics resources "Vital Records Information," be prepared to answer questions in Step 3.

Please be careful to not click on the advertising banners. The information in the Vital Records Information site is indexing and basic annotation of the sources for vital records in each state in the U.S. and many countries. It is not the full and complete information for your state or country. Click on the link to your state or country's vital records agencies and read the information available on your state or country's site. Note: Many agencies do not provide an online order form for records, but they may subscribe to a commercial service called "VitalCheck," which will do so. Read carefully to see if records are available through "VitalCheck" for your state.

STEP 1.   Connect to *http://vitalrec.com/index.html*
STEP 2.   Use the map option. Click on your state on the map.
STEP 3.   1. Does your state have a searchable index to any vital records online?

❑ Yes   ❑ No

2. Can you order records online?

❑ Yes   ❑ No

3. What kinds of information did you find for state?
STEP 4.   If you found a searchable index or full-text of vital records in your state, please connect there and try a search. Describe what you found.

Note: If you are working self-paced and would like instructor feedback e-mail your responses and questions to *diane@kovacs.com*

Activity 2.3.   Searching the FamilySearch and American Family Immigration History Center Databases

Overview:

In this activity you will connect to the LDS Family History Research Site. This is a complete online collection of some of the indexes that have been available in the LDS Family History Research Centers on CD-ROM or microfilm. The databases contain the indexing for documents held by the LDS Library, as well as some of the family history records compiled by church members.

Read carefully in STEP 1 to learn how to obtain document copies from the LDS Library and also the value and limitations of this database in careful genealogical research. REMEMBER that this database is an index and pointer to particular documents. You will need to order copies of these documents to prove connections in genealogical research.

If possible, you will also connect to the Ellis Island Records database.

STEP 1.   Connect to *http://www.familysearch.org*. Click on the "Library" Tab and read carefully through the information provided. Especially take note of the databases described under "Key Resources." Also, click "Record Collections." Note that the online databases are not the actual copies of the genealogical records held at the LDS Libraries. Read the "Frequently Asked Questions." Read the information on "Services" to learn how to obtain copies of the records held by the LDS Libraries.

STEP 2.   Click on the "Search" tab. Look over the options for searching. Enter your search including as much information as you have available, but be prepared to use the minimal amount of information required in each search.

STEP 3.   Click on "Ancestral Search." Use the surname ENGELBRECHT and look for Albert ENGELBRECHT. Note that if you search on a last name only you can only then also search on COUNTRY. You can look for Marriage/Death & Birth Records in particular. Return to the Ancestral Search screen and Type in a family name of your choice. Did you locate information about your ancestor? Please note that your ancestor need not have been a member of the LDS church.

STEP 4.   Use your browser to try connecting to the Ellis Island Records database at the American Family Immigration History Center *http://www.ellisislandrecords.org/*. Note: Due to the extreme popularity of this site it may not be possible to connect immediately.

STEP 5.   Use this search tool to locate ancestors known to have emigrated to the United States between 1892 and 1924 through Ellis Island. Remember that this database does not contain all of those records as some were lost or unavailable. Many people also came to the U.S. prior to or after these dates. Still more came through other U.S. ports of entry or across the Canadian or Mexican borders. See the NARA Web site *http://www.nara.gov/genealogy* for information about retrieving those records if there are any.

Note: If you are working self-paced and would like instructor feedback e-mail your responses and questions to *diane@kovacs.com*

Activity 2.4.   Using and Comparing the RootsWeb, Cyndi's List, and the SurnameWeb Metasites

Overview:

In this activity you will evaluate and compare three genealogical reference metasites: RootsWeb, which searches all the genealogy Web sites registered with the RootsWeb Cooperative; Cyndi's List, which is the most comprehensive compilation of genealogical Web sites; and SurnameWeb, which is a search engine that searches an extensive index of genealogy Web sites among other features.

STEP 1.	Connect to **RootsWeb** *http://www.rootsweb.com*. Read through the contents of this main page. Especially look at "Exploring RootsWeb." Scroll back up to "Search RootsWeb.com" and click on "Index of all Databases." Read through these. Then click back to the main page again.
STEP 2.	Click the cursor in the search form under "Search RootsWeb.com." Type in a family name of your choice or search on ENGELBRECHT, which will retrieve results. Click on the "Submit" button. You may also browse alphabetically.
STEP 3.	Click through the retrieved links that you find. What kind of sites are you connecting to? Read carefully the pages that are displayed so you can identify which RootsWeb database or outside source you are reading from.
STEP 4.	Did you find any individuals whom you recognize as being related to you or the person whose family name you searched for?
STEP 5.	Now connect to Cyndi's list at *http://www.cyndislist.com*. Read carefully through this main page to understand the scope and purpose of this collection. You will need to scroll down several screens to find the actual categories of Web site listings. Look for the area "Main Category Listings," "No Frills Category..." and browse through these. Notice the "Search It!" option. You will need to scroll down again to use the search forms in this heading.
STEP 6.	Choose a category in which you are interested or search for a topic area or surname. What category or search did you choose? What kinds of sites and information are you finding? Look at the Title bar and Location box in your Web browser to see the site names and the URLs when you follow different links.
STEP 7.	Describe what you found in RootsWeb compared to what you found in Cyndi's List.

STEP 8.   Connect to the **SurnameWeb** site *http://www.surnameweb.com*. Read carefully through this site to learn the scope and purpose of SurnameWeb. Click on "Help" to learn more. Click back to the main SurnameWebpage

STEP 9.   Click on the "Search" option and search for a family name of your choice. If possible use the same family name as you used for the RootsWeb search in Steps 1-4 above. What kind of results do you retrieve? Click through and look at some of your results. Look at the Title bar and Location box in your Web browser to see the site names and the URLs when you follow the links.

STEP 10.   Did you find any individuals whom you recognize as being related to you or the person whose family name you searched for?

STEP 11.   Describe what you found in SurnameWeb as compared to RootsWeb and Cyndi's List.

Note: If you are working self-paced and would like instructor feedback e-mail your responses and questions to *diane@kovacs.com*

Activity 2.5.   Exploring The USGenWeb Project

Overview:

In this activity you will search for vital records and statistics sites for your state. Using the USGenWeb site for your state and county, be prepared to answer questions in Step 4.

STEP 1.   Connect to http://www.usgenweb.com/

STEP 2.   Read through the "Special Projects" and other information, then go back to the main page and click on "The Project's State Pages" link. Use the Map option to click on the state of Idaho, then use the list of counties and click on "Bonner" county. Who is the county GenWeb coordinator? What projects are the Bonner County Idaho USGenWeb volunteers working on?

STEP 3.   Go back to the USGenWeb main page and click on "The Project's State Pages" link. Use the Map option to click on a state of your choice, then choose a county.

Please note that your county may have many detailed projects or even absolutely nothing—or some quantity in between. If you don't find something for the state and county you chose, it is not because you've done something wrong. Try looking for a different state or county and see how different they can be. Remember that USGenWeb is all volunteer projects.

STEP 4.   1. Does your state and/or county have a Genweb Project?

❑ Yes   ❑ No

2. What kinds of information did you find for your state and/or county? Did you look for another state or county? How did that state/county compare to Bonner County Idaho that you looked at in STEP 2?

3. Who is the county GenWeb coordinator for the county you chose?

Note: If you are working self-paced and would like instructor feedback e-mail your responses and questions to *diane@kovacs.com*

Activity 2.6. Comparing Ancestry.com and FamilyTreeMaker.com

Overview:

In this activity you will connect to and compare two commercial suppliers of genealogical data sources. Their Web sites provide indexes to those genealogical data sources. Ancestry.com provides many of their data sources full text online. Familytreemaker.com provides most of their data sources on CD-Rom or other computer files. However, they also inform the searcher of sources of information that are available elsewhere. Both provide a certain amount of data free. Both host a version of the free database of Social Security Death Records. The Social Security Death Records are an excellent first-step tool for locating and then ordering information about recently deceased (within the last two decades approximately) family members.

STEP 1.   Connect to http://www.ancestry.com. Read through the options on the screen. These change frequently.

STEP 2.   Click on the Search tab and take a minute to look at the option "Images Online." Ancestry.com is putting census data images online. This is one of their subscriber services.

Now click back and use the Search tool to search for some names of your choice. Note the variety of databases you retrieve. Which ones are free for you to access? What kinds of information do the free databases provide? Look at the free ones, especially the Social Security Death Records database. What kinds of information do you get?

STEP 3.   Connect to http:/www.familytreemaker.com. Read through the options on the screen. These change frequently. Repeat STEP 2 in this database. What is the main difference between these two Web sites?

Note: If you are working self-paced and would like instructor feedback e-mail your responses and questions to *diane@kovacs.com*

Activity 2.7.   Locating a Family Name in the GENDEX—Index to Family History Web Pages and the RootsWeb World Connect Database

Overview:

In this activity you will compare results of searching for a family name in the GENDEX—WWW Genealogy Index and with the RootsWeb World Connect Database.

STEP 1.	Connect to http://www.gendex.com/gendex/. Click on the information links and read through them. Especially look at "How to contact the contributor of a particular piece of information you find in the index." Click on "Access the Index" then on "surname index."
STEP 2.	Click the cursor in the the search form. Type in a family name of your choice or search on ENGELBRECHT, which will retrieve results. Click on the "Submit" button. You may also browse alphabetically.
STEP 3.	Click through the name links that you find. What kind of sites are you connecting to. Look at the Title bar and Location box in your Web browser to see the site names and the URLs when you follow different name links
STEP 4.	Did you find any individuals whom you recognize as being related to you or the person whose family name you searched for?
	❏ Yes ❏ No
	For example: Engelbrecht is my birth name. Most of my family lives in Northern Illinois and Wisconsin. I find several Engelbrechts that I recognize.
STEP 5.	Who provided the information for the individuals whose records you clicked through on?

Note: If you are working self-paced and would like instructor feedback e-mail your responses and questions to *diane@kovacs.com*

Activity 2.8. Browsing the United States Historical Census Data Browser

Overview:

In this activity you will learn about the United States Historical Census Data Browser at the University of Virginia Library site http://fisher.lib.virginia.edu/census/ in cooperation with the Inter-university Consortium for Political and Social Research (ICPSR) www.icpsr.umich.edu/. Then we will look at the USGenWeb Census Project.

Please keep in mind that your state may have still been a territory or other geographic unit during any given census. The far western states for example may not be in a pre-1890 census. For example, Colorado would be in the 1880 census as it became a state in 1876, but Arizona would not be in a census until 1910 as it became a state in 1912. I recommend www.50states.com/ for quick state facts and also county maps if you are interested.

STEP 1.   Use your Web browser to connect to the United States Historical Census Data Browser http://fisher.lib.virginia.edu/census/. Read the overview of this site on this first page.

STEP 2.   Click on the "1850" census button, then select the category "Libraries." Select as many statistics as you are interested in. Hold down the shift key (MAC OS) or the ctrl key (Windows) to select multiple statistics.

STEP 3.   Scroll down and then click on the "Browse 1850 data" button to view the statistics you have chosen.

STEP 4.   On the statisics view page scroll down and select "Ohio" then click on the "View Counties" button. E-mail the instructor diane@kovacs.com and report the library statistics for Ohio. Then select your state and find the statistics for your county, if there are any. If your state was not a state in 1850 try a later census year.

STEP 5.   Choose a census year and statistics of your choice and repeat steps 2-4—guided by the options available for each statistic—until you feel confident of using this tool.

STEP 6   Connect to USGenWeb http://www.usgenweb.org and click on USGenWeb Project Archives, then click on Census Images. First look to see what is available for the state of Texas in Cass County. Then look for information on a state and county of your choice. What Census images, if any, did you find for each county?

Note: If you are working self-paced and would like instructor feedback e-mail your responses and questions to *diane@kovacs.com*

Part 3
How to Network with Living Family Members and/or Fellow Genealogical Researchers

> "When I run a genealogy, I go to the courthouse for the real evidence that I can use as proof. But first I try to find somebody who knows what the facts are, more or less, so I'll have something to start on"(Landrum, 1992:66).
>
> ... "Of course after Ella had given me all the information she could remember, I went to the library. Most of my dates, etc., I got from obituaries, because although most of the Drovers lived away from the border country, they still made a noise in the Banner-Democrat when they died" (Landrum, 1992:77).

This part discusses the use of the Internet for communications between family members and researchers and using the Internet to plan for offline correspondence and travel.

Finding Your Living Family Members and/or Fellow Genealogical Researchers

Generally, there are three types of Web site or other Internet tools where you may find living family members and/or fellow genealogical researchers:

- Family members doing genealogical research publish their research on the Web.
- Genealogical researchers gather in online communities to chat, participate in Web boards (threaded discussions), newsgroups, or communicate through e-mail discussion lists.
- Formally, nationally or locally, genealogical researchers network through genealogical or historical organizations and societies.

The first type—personal family history pages—is fairly straightforward to search. Any Web search tool can be used to search for family genealogy Web sites. Search using a surname along with the keywords "genealogy," "genea-

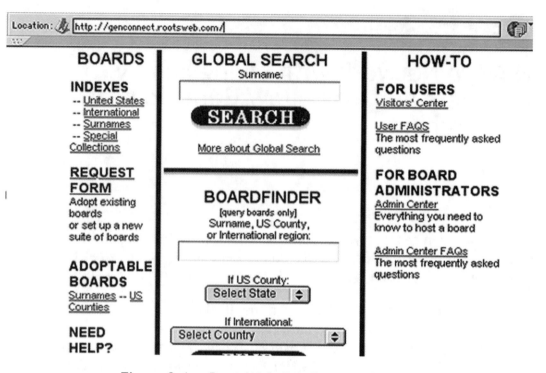

Figure 3.1.   RootsWeb GenConnect Search

logical," "family history," and the like, as well as a state, province, or county name to narrow the search. The Web search tools Google (www.google.com) and Altavista (www.altavista.com) have been particularly useful for finding family genealogy Web pages. Using Google, simply type the surname then one or more keywords including a state, province, or county name. Using Altavista, the proximity operator NEAR can be very powerful, e.g., "Finch near genealogy." Including a state or county name will help to narrow your search e.g., (Finch near genealogy) and Illinois.

Living family members may also be located on the Internet by doing a simple search for e-mail addresses, or even postal addresses and telephone numbers. Many search tools will also do telephone and address look-up. Good examples of such tools include Yahoo!'s People Finder (www.people.yahoo.com), WhoWhere? (www.whowhere.com), AnyWho (www.anywho.com), the Internet Address Finder (www.iaf.net), or Bigfoot (www.bigfoot.com), just to mention some of the most popular of such tools.

Most of the sites discussed in Part 2 also provide search tools for finding living family members who are fellow genealogical researchers. RootsWeb is the most powerful of these. RootsWeb hosts the GenSeeker (http://seeker.rootsweb.com/search.html), the GenConnect Global Surname Search (http://genconnect.rootsweb.com), and WorldConnect (http://worldconnect.rootsweb.com/) projects, as well as thousands of discussion lists (mailing lists), Web boards, and chat listings. The GenSeeker tool is used to

---

**Success Story 3.1   Pursuing Old Family Stories
Through the Web**

Beth A. Stahr, MLS, CGRS <bstahr@i-55.com> or <bstahr@selu.edu> (Trustee and Treasurer of the Board for Certification of Genealogists and Vice President of the Louisiana Genealogical and Historical Society)

Several years ago I posted on one of the Texas counties query pages of USGenWeb. A very distant cousin replied. She is descended from a younger sister of my great-great-grandmother, Malinda Caroline Price Chowning. Malinda had an illegitimate son, Claude Duval Price, born circa 1872. She eventually married Uriah Chowning in Texas, with whom she had twin daughters, Ada and Ida. She remained close to her twins, but was not very close to my great-grandfather, Claude. I felt that I would never learn any further information about this situation.

However, the woman who responded to my query knew of the situation. Isn't it just like the younger sisters to gossip about the misfortune of their oldest sister? The story of Malinda's unfortunate situation was carried down through the generations, and the family even knew Claude's name and that he had left Texas for the Indian Territory. According to family tradition, Malinda was engaged to a Methodist circuit rider in northwestern Georgia or southern Tennessee where the Prices lived. When the preacher learned of her "condition," he left and never returned, as it wouldn't be proper for a man in his position to marry a young woman with child.

The entire family, including some of Malinda's already married siblings, packed their belongings and moved to Texas, out of embarrassment. This is an interesting story, with some possible opportunity for research. Without meeting that distant cousin on USGenWeb, I'd never know the story!

search for the Web sites hosted by or registered with RootsWeb. The GenConnect Global Surname Search (Figure 3.1) searches the entire collection of RootsWeb hosted discussions for queries or comments about a given name, family, or keyword.

Several sites offer volunteers who will help with look-ups for materials they own or have easily accessible to them physically. RootsWeb's "Random Acts of Genealogical Kindness" project (http://raogk.rootsweb.com/) and the Genealogy Helplist project (www.helplist.org) are two volunteer groups. The Web sites list the contact information for the volunteers and what books or databases in which they will do look-ups.

At some point you or your patron may want to locate a professional genealogical researcher to assist in your research. You or your patron may also

---

Success Story 3.2   Finding My Cousin and Sharing Our Family History Research Online

James Swan jswan@ckls.org (Author of *The Librarian's Guide to Genealogical Research*)

In 1996 I put my actively searching surname list on RootsWeb Interactive Surname List (http://rsl.rootsweb.com/cgi-bin/rslsql.cgi).

This is my listing: Page 1800 to 1995 VT>IL>FtMadison,IA>CA, USA jswan. If you are not familiar with this site get to know it. It is really powerful for bringing those who are searching the same lines together.

Go there and type in the surname PAGE and use IA for Iowa as the location. When I first tried the search I found three other listings; none of which matched anything I had. About every three months I would check it again. One day the list came up with the listing put up by Bob Campbell. This is his listing: Page c1800 1883 VT>FtMadison,IA,USA campbelr

I checked his list of surnames and found: Martin c1752 1879 Lebanon,CT>FtMadison,IA,USA   campbelr Page c1800 1883 VT>FtMadison,IA,USA campbelr

My listing for Martin. Martin 1700 1879 CT>Columbus,OH>FtMadison,IA,USA jswan

When I saw his Martin and Page together I knew we had a match. John Page and Mary Lavinia Martin married 1856 in Ft. Madison, Iowa.

I sent him via e-mail a short query outlining the information I had on the family and requested any information he had. In about 20 minutes I received a reply that started, "Hi Cousin." His great-grandmother and my great-grandfather were brother and sister. He was able to send me an obituary for my great-grandfather, Charles Page and was able to give me the maiden name of John Page's mother. We are still looking for his father.

---

want to become a professional genealogical researcher. Two Web sites provide information that will help connect the researcher with a qualified professional genealogical researcher and also provide background information and training opportunities for those who want to become qualified professional genealogical researchers. The Association of Professional Genealogists (www.apgen.org) Web site has a directory of members. Information about qualifying to join this organization is provided. Links to other related organizations are included. Board for Certification of Genealogists (www.bcgcertification.org/) provides a "Roster of BCG Certified Individuals" and a comprehensive overview of how to become a BCG Certified Genealogist. This site also links to other related organizations.

Exploring Genealogical Discussion Lists, Newsgroups, Web Boards, and Chats

There are literally tens of thousands of discussion lists for genealogical research. Most online or e-mail discussions are focused on a specific surname. The RootsWeb site hosts many of the oldest and most useful of these, in addition to hosting Web boards and chats on genealogical topics. In Activity 3.2, you'll look at some of the RootsWeb communication tools. UsGenWeb (www.usgenweb.org) and the WorldGenWeb projects among other RootsWeb-sponsored projects also host genealogical discussions and Web boards. Two genealogical research "Success Stories" describing how genealogical researchers Beth Stahr and James Swan have successfully used discussion lists and Web boards in their research are narrated in this part.

Another good site to look for genealogical discussion lists and Usenet newsgroups is the "Genealogy Resources on the Internet" site (www.rootsweb.com/~jfuller/gen_mail.html).

The best discussion list for librarians working with genealogical researchers is Genealib. The "Librarians Serving Genealogists" homepage (www.cas.usf.edu/lis/genealib/) provides information about subscribing to Genealib and searching the archives.

Many of the commercial sites such as Ancestry.com (www.ancestry.com), FamilyTreeMaker (www.familytreemaker.com), and SurnameWeb (www.surnameweb.com) also host Web boards or discussion lists.

Using E-mail to Communicate, Netiquette, and Asking the Right Questions

When e-mailing queries or sharing information with others it is important to follow some basic rules of netiquette and to ask the right kinds of questions. The Six Core Rules of Netiquette:

1. When participating in discussion lists and newsgroups, keep your questions and comments relevant to the focus of the discussion topic. Read the overview of the group's purpose and read the postings for a time before posting yourself.
2. Resist the temptation to "flame" others on discussion lists or newsgroups. "To flame" means to send messages that show anger inappropriately, make derogatory statements, or otherwise threaten or demean the recipient. Treat other people on the Internet as you would want them to treat you.
3. Be professional and careful in your messages. Use correct grammar and spelling as you would in paper correspondence. Remember that what you say about others or any given topic is not private in e-mail. E-mail is easily forwarded and frequently printed.

4. Be careful when using sarcasm and humor. There is no clear way of conveying those subtle nuances and the reader may be very offended.
5. NEVER forward chain letters or send out mass e-mailings (SPAM) to individual correspondents or to discussion or mailing lists. The latter may ban you if you do so.
6. Notify your correspondent and ask for permission before sending file attachments. Provide the name of the attachment and the size. Do not send file attachments to discussion or mailing lists.

In the excellent workshops she teaches, Cyndi Howells (the creator of Cyndi's List), recommends typing surnames in ALL CAPS, and providing your correspondent with only the information required to answer your question, or to answer their question. Don't provide them with your entire family history unless you are asked for this. Don't be impatient about getting a response. Remember that everyone has a life in addition to their e-mail.

The National Genealogical Society Web site (www.nsgenealogy.org) publishes "Standards for Sharing Information with Others." It is reproduced with the permission of the National Genealogical Society:

"Standards For Sharing Information With Others

Recommended by the National Genealogical Society

Conscious of the fact that sharing information or data with others, whether through speech, documents or electronic media, is essential to family history research and that it needs continuing support and encouragement, responsible family historians consistently—

- respect the restrictions on sharing information that arise from the rights of another as an author, originator or compiler; as a living private person; or as a party to a mutual agreement.
- observe meticulously the legal rights of copyright owners, copying or distributing any part of their works only with their permission, or to the limited extent specifically allowed under the law's "fair use" exceptions.
- identify the sources for all ideas, information and data from others, and the form in which they were received, recognizing that the unattributed use of another's intellectual work is plagiarism.
- respect the authorship rights of senders of letters, electronic mail and data files, forwarding or disseminating them further only with the sender's permission.
- inform people who provide information about their families as to the ways it may be used, observing any conditions they impose and respect-

---

ing any reservations they may express regarding the use of particular items.

- require some evidence of consent before assuming that living people are agreeable to further sharing of information about themselves.
- convey personal identifying information about living people—like age, home address, occupation or activities—only in ways that those concerned have expressly agreed to.
- recognize that legal rights of privacy may limit the extent to which information from publicly available sources may be further used, disseminated or published.
- communicate no information to others that is known to be false, or without making reasonable efforts to determine its truth, particularly information that may be derogatory.
- are sensitive to the hurt that revelations of criminal, immoral, bizarre or irresponsible behavior may bring to family members."

©2000 by National Genealogical Society. Permission is granted to copy or publish this material provided it is reproduced in its entirety, including this notice.
Committees § Standards (www.ngsgenealogy.org/comstandsharing.htm).

The Internet is an ideal communications tool for interviewing your family members about what they know of your family relationships, sharing genealogical data with your fellow researchers, or for learning more from genealogical experts. It is ideal **if** the people you want to communicate with have access to and use the Internet. Activity 3.1 is a guide for planning to interview your living family members. Use Activity 1.2 to plan your questions. Using e-mail for these interviews has several advantages:

1. No long distance phone charges.
2. Recorded electronic text version of both your questions and the answers.
3. Very little time delay compared with postal mailed questions and answers.

For example, when starting to research the Finch/Wilson/Schumm families, I began by e-mailing my mother. I asked her everything that she remembered about her family. In some things she was mistaken—she thought that the Wilsons had come from Germany as had the Schumms—but she was able to supply me with many details of names and birth places. I discovered that she had a box of obituary clippings that she postal mailed to me. These clippings greatly simplified my initial search on the Internet by providing names, dates, and countries of origins for the Schumms and for Caroline Wilson (Lovell) my great-great-grandmother. These obituaries did contain some very small errors of fact, for example, that John Schumm had come to Dixon, Illinois in 1880 when in fact he'd lived in Sterling, Illinois from 1880-1892; and Elsie Dunn (Schumm) was listed as L.C. By using e-mail communications with my mother, I was able to correct some of the errors and identify sources of further information. For example, when I searched for my Grandma "Anna" Wilson (Schumm) in the Social Security Death Index through Ancestry.com, I understood that her name was "Anna" from my mother, and from copies of obituaries for her husband, mother, father, and mother-in-law. I also knew she had received Social Security benefits because my mother had assisted her to complete the forms back in the mid-1960s. However, I could not find any Social Security Death record information for Anna Wilson in the state of Illinois. I e-mailed my mother about this. Mom revealed that although everyone called her Anna, Grandma Wilson's name was really Ann. With the correct spelling I found her record easily and ordered her benefits application form copy from the Social Security Administration. This application contained her parents' names, her birth date, birthplace, and other helpful information.

The Internet is international, and international genealogical research can be greatly simplified by the communications factor of the Internet. This example prefigures topics discussed in Part 4, but illustrates how Internet communication facilitates international genealogical research. In researching my husband's maternal grandparents Kacsandy/Kacsandi, we found some information about the origins and background of the Kacsandy/Kacsandi surname on the Internet that was written in Hungarian (Magya'rul). When we e-mailed the site's Webmaster to ask if there was an English version of some of the Kacsandy/Kacsandi materials, she translated the main document into English and e-mailed it to us! This information indicated that Kacsandi meant the person was from the village of Kacsand. Using historical maps of Hungary—found through the WorldGenWeb site (http://worldgenweb.org) by linking through the EastEuropeGenWeb site (www.rootsweb.com/~easeurgw/) to the HungaryGenWeb site (www.rootsweb.com/~wghungar/)—we located the Hungarian village that was called Kacsand before World War I. That area of Hungary was affected drastically by the Treaty of Trianon (see http://newmedia.cgu.edu/petropoulos/arrow/history/worldwar.html for the basics) and became part of Slovakia, now the Slovak Republic, and took the Slovak name Kacanov. We used the WorldGenWeb pages for Hungary (www.rootsweb.com/~wghungar/) and the Slovak Republic (www.rootsweb.com/~svkwgw/) to locate both the historical and modern maps and make a city by city comparison, to confirm that Kacanov was the same village as Kacsand.

A last tip for e-mail netiquette concerning correspondence with individuals you do not know personally: Be patient. It may be weeks or months before those individuals have time to reply to your message or even logon to check their e-mail. Many people whom I have e-mailed concerning surnames in which they have expressed an interest in discussion lists or Web boards have never replied to my notes sharing my data or asking them for theirs. Many people have replied. Remember that for many researchers, genealogy is their recreation or hobby and not their full-time job. Remember that many researchers are volunteers and treat them respectfully.

Communicating with Your Non-Internet Connected Family Members

Many researchers and family members do not yet use the Internet. For example, in my own family research I can exchange e-mail with my mother to query her about her side of my family. However, I must use the telephone to speak with my paternal grandmother, and postal mail to correspond with my great-uncle who is compiling the genealogy for my paternal grandmother's family. In designing my first "Genealogy Research on the Internet" workshop I demonstrated the genealogical research tools that were then available on the Internet using my own family names as examples. One major problem I had was the commonness of my family surnames. There were just too many examples, and most of the examples I found were not for members of my family. In order to try to identify unique family names to use for the demonstrations, I spent hours on the telephone with my paternal grandmother who lives in Illinois where I grew up. During those discussions, I learned from her, for the first time, that her family originated in the same area of southern Ohio as the Ohio Valley Area Libraries (OVAL) audience for whom I was presenting. One of the unique family names I learned of is "Cattee." One of the librarians in my first audience was Betsy Dement of the Portsmouth, Ohio Public Library Genealogical Dept. (one of the most knowledgeable genealogy librarians I've ever spoken with). During a class break, Betsy approached me to tell me that one of her regular summer visitors was a gentleman from Iowa who researched the family name "Cattee." She asked my permission to give him my telephone number and address. Within a few days the gentleman she referred to telephoned me. The gentleman was my great-uncle, my paternal grandmother's younger brother. He had already done a significant part of our family genealogy. Knowing that he had done all that work, rather than having to start from scratch, I can ask him for all of his notes and records from years of work and travel. However, he is not on the Internet and is not likely to be. Further, all of his records are on paper and there are no computer files to share. Much good genealogy information remains to be published on the Web in the future by a new generation of genealogical researchers taking up the trail from their family researchers.

Using the Internet to Plan Your Genealogical Research Correspondence and Travel

One of the most valuable aspects of the Internet is that it provides tools that genealogical researchers can use to plan their travel itinerary or plan their correspondence. Serious genealogical researchers will almost always have to travel or correspond with genealogical and historical societies, libraries, archives, museums, cemeteries, churches, courthouses, and other organizations. These places that hold genealogical research related records and documents frequently have Web sites on which they publish basic information about their physical location. Important information for the genealogical researcher planning travel or correspondence includes information such as contact addresses, scope and contents of the collection, hours when the organization will receive researchers, terms of use of materials, fees for research services, and a variety of other helpful information. Some sites are beginning to publish scanned images or transcriptions of the genealogical records they hold.

Once the genealogical researcher decides to travel, the Internet also provides some good tools to use in planning their itineraries and even purchasing air, train, or boat tickets, renting cars, and finding and reserving a place to stay.

Genealogical and Historical Societies and Organizations

Genealogical and historical societies have provided networking opportunities for centuries before the advent of the Internet. Thousands of local, regional, national, and international organizations exist in support of genealogical research. These organizations continue to form a backbone for educating genealogical researchers, and a focus for archiving and recording genealogical research. Many of these solid sources of support and information have a presence on the Internet. It is possible to connect to the National Genealogical Society Web site (www.ngsgenealogy.org), apply and pay for membership, register for an online genealogical researcher beginners course, register for an extensive genealogical research continuing education correspondence course, read the news, learn about conferences, research events, and much much more. Some organizations are digitizing their archives and research collections and making them available on the Web. The International Internet Genealogical Society (IIGS) (www.iigs.org/) and the Ohio Historical Society (www.ohiohistory.org/) are two examples of organizations building digital collections of scanned and indexed historical documents, newspapers, manuscripts, and vital records. The IIGS projects are multi-national and include projects for Canada, Ecuador, and the Irish Genealogical project Genuki among others.

Many local and regional genealogical and historical societies and organizations are also involved with RootsWeb and the USGenWeb projects. Some society and organization Web sites are hosted by RootsWeb. A listing of these is online at www.rootsweb.com/~Websites/gensoc.html.

It is also fruitful to use the Society Hall Web site (www.familyhistory.com/societyhall/) or the Federation of Genealogical Societies (www.fgs.org/) Web site to identify local, regional, national, or international organizations that might be useful to you or your patrons.

"Society Hall" is a Web site collaboration between Ancestry.com and the Federation of Genealogical Societies (FGS). It is a nearly comprehensive directory of genealogical and historical societies that have a Web presence. These genealogical and historical society Web sites can be used as finding tools to locate and search locally held genealogical collections, as well as to provide genealogical researchers with supportive affiliations. Many societies also publish newsletters online and even provide online genealogical research training and continuing education opportunities.

The Federation of Genealogical Societies (FGS) "is a non-profit organization comprised of hundreds of genealogical and historical societies, family associations, and libraries with a combined membership of over 500,000 members. FGS is actively involved in efforts to protect societies, facilitate and coordinate society activities, and monitor events significant to the genealogical community. The Federation is the collective voice for genealogists at the national level. The FGS Member Symbol identifies all societies in the Hall that belong to FGS" (Federation of Genealogical Societies, 2001).

Genealogical societies and organizations frequently maintain archives and libraries. Many have searchable catalogs, as well as information about their visitor services, location, and hours on their Web sites. This can be a great asset for the researcher. For example, for my research I need to get access to the 1830 and 1840 U.S. Censuses for Connecticut. In these census records I hope to find information about my great-great-grandfather Gilbert P. Finch, who according to the 1880 Census Images for Amboy, Illinois (searched via Ancestry.com) was born in Connecticut in 1831. I could travel to Connecticut and visit the Connecticut State Library or one of their historical or genealogical societies. The Connecticut State Library Web site at www.cslib.org/handg.htm provides me with all the information I need to decide where and when to visit them; whether they have the census records I need; as well as links to the Connecticut historical and genealogical societies' Web sites. Or perhaps I might find a holding library or archive closer to where I live. I searched RootsWeb to locate a URL for the Western Reserve Historical Society that I know is located less than an hour's drive from me. RootsWeb located a page on their site that contains a profile of the policies and collections, as well as the URL for the library. The profile describes the collection as including the census microforms I require. For $30 per hour I can ask the librarians there to browse the census microforms for me. Connecting to the Western Reserve Historical Society Library Web site (www.wrhs.org/) I can obtain the hours and admission fee for general visitors and can plan to drive up to Cleveland for a day or so.

Libraries, Archives, Museums, and Monuments

When I was an academic reference librarian, I sometimes had difficulty with genealogical researchers who came to the library with certain little "how-to-do" genealogy books in hand. Some of these seemed to say that the researcher should just go to the nearest large library and they would have everything needed to complete the researcher's entire genealogy: census records, birth and death and marriage records, cemetery records, and so on. Many libraries, even large libraries, don't have all of those things and if they do, they have them for the local area or special interest areas only. The real question that the researcher needs to have answered is which libraries have the materials they need. Then they'll need to know if they can find those materials online, can order copies, or will have to travel to the location to search and copy materials.

I felt bad having to say no to the genealogists because my library (Kent State University) didn't have vital records of any kind, although they did have published genealogies, journals, and an extensive special collections including the May 4th collection, the Ohio First Ladies collection, and more.

In those days, I always had to refer people to other libraries, historical societies, or local government offices, not knowing whether those libraries did in fact have the materials my patrons were requesting, unless I telephoned on my patron's behalf.

Librarians and the genealogical researchers they work with can use the Internet to find out where they really need to visit to get the records, find the people they need to talk to, the addresses they need to order documents. Occasionally, they may find some real genealogical data online that can be used to start or further their research.

The following Web sites are some of the best sources for online full-text materials—e-libraries and e-archives, directories of libraries, archives, museums, monuments, etc. The section which follows the e-archives presents a selection of some of the best genealogical library or archive Web sites. The first mention, however, goes to a printed treasure.

Thomas Kemp's book *The Genealogist's Virtual Library: Full-text Books on the World Wide Web* (2000) is an essential starting place for anyone looking for full-text genealogical books on the Internet. The book comes with a CD-ROM that can be loaded on any computer. The entire book is on the CD-ROM in pdf (Adobe Acrobat) format and the URLs for the full-text book sites are clickable.

Success Story 3.3 How the Making of America Project Records Helped Solve a Family Puzzle

Carol Taylor ctaylor@ci.greenville.tx.us (Librarian for Genealogy/Local History W. Walworth Harrison Public Library Greenville, Texas)

I am currently writing a biographical sketch on a great-great-grandfather who fought in both the Confederate and Union Armies in the Civil War. I wanted to determine the probable cause of his changing sides. From his military service records I knew the Confederate unit he was in, that he was a prisoner of war at Camp Douglas, that he was in the prisoner exchange in Vicksburg in the fall of 1862, and that he was mustered out in October of 1862. He joined a Federal cavalry unit in Tennessee in October of 1863 in Nashville and served until the end of the war. In May of 1864, he returned to northern Alabama to marry the widow of one of his Confederate comrades in arms.

None of the combined military records or regimental histories were enough to help me understand the reasoning behind his choices. I went to the Official Records of the War of the Rebellion at library5.library.cornell.edu/moa/ moa_browse.html (Cornell University's Making of America project main page at http://library5.library.cornell.edu/moa/) for the digitized copy of the 127 volumes in this series. The original 127 volumes were rather obliquely indexed. Less than 200 copies of the Official Records were published. Original copies are rather difficult to find. This Web site presents these original records in a usable manner consistent with good genealogical research methods.

Using a Boolean Search, I was able to discover that my ancestor was at Fort Donelson on the Tennessee/Kentucky border. I was able to read the original reports after the Confederate defeat and understand that General Pillow and General Floyd escaped with their elite troops, leaving the remainder of the troops and General Buckner to surrender to the Federals. According to the Official Records, some 15,000 to 20,000 Confederate soldiers were taken prisoners and transported to Camp Douglas. My ancestor was 15 years old at the time. While at Camp Douglas, he was in the prison hospital on two different occasions. The Official Records gave an insight into the prison hospital and the care of patients. After the exchange of prisoners at Vicksburg, my ancestor made his way back home to northern Alabama.

In the fall of 1863, he joined the Fifth Tennessee Cavalry. Once again, I did a Boolean Search for "Fifth" and "Tennessee" to discover that this unit was just across the state line in southeastern Tennessee. Using combined military service records and the Official Records of the War of the Rebellion I was able to piece together the probable events in my ancestor's war time experience. The amazing fact is that he is never mentioned by name. The details are there for anyone taking the time and patience to find them.

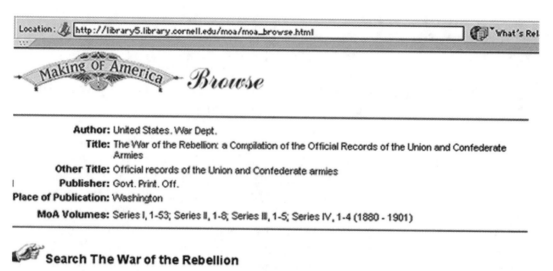

Figure 3.2. Making of America Project Page for *The War of the Rebellion: a Compilation of the Official Records of the Union and Confederate Armies*.

E-Archives

The Making of America (MoA) project is a collaborative effort of the University of Michigan (http://moa.umdl.umich.edu) and Cornell University (http://library5.library.cornell.edu/moa). The MoA project is funded by the Andrew W. Mellon Foundation. Librarians, instructors, and scholars at the University of Michigan and Cornell University are scanning historical documents, books, serials, pictures, and more and making them searchable, browseable and accessible in images on the Internet.

"Making of America (MoA) is a digital library of primary sources in American social history from the antebellum period through reconstruction. The collection is particularly strong in the subject areas of education, psychology, American history, sociology, religion, and science and technology. The collection currently contains approximately 8,500 books and 50,000 journal articles with 19th century imprints . . . The Making of America collection is made up of images of the pages in the books and journals. When you find something you want to look at, you will see a scanned image of the actual pages of the 19th century volume" (Making of America, 2001).

One of the most valuable parts of this project in terms of genealogical research is located on the Cornell University's Making of America Web site (http://library5.library.cornell.edu/moa/). The multi-volume monographs: *Official Records of the Union and Confederate Navies in the War of the Re-*

bellion (1894 - 1922) and *The War of the Rebellion: a Compilation of the Official Records of the Union and Confederate Armies (1880 - 1901)* (Figure 3.2) contain much information that can be used to locate and identify ancestors who may have participated at some level during the U.S. Civil War.

Library and Archives Web Sites

Cyndi's List includes library and archive Web sites selected for their genealogical research value. Use Cyndi's List (www.CyndisList.com/), and search under the category "Libraries, Archives & Museums General Library Sites."

Terry Abraham (tabraham@uidaho.edu) of the University of Idaho Library Special Collections (www.uidaho.edu/special-collections/Other.Repositories.html) maintains an International directory of Web sites for libraries, archives, and other organizations that are sources of primary documents:

"A listing of over 4700 Web sites describing holdings of manuscripts, archives, rare books, historical photographs, and other primary sources for the research scholar. All links have been tested for correctness and appropriateness" (University of Idaho Library Special Collections, 2001). Most of these Web sites have catalogs of the materials held and sometimes access to digitized collections or ordering information for document copies.

Chris and Thomas M. Tinney, Sr. maintain the Web site "Archives and Knowledge Management Scholarly Online Resource Evidence and Records for use by Genealogists and Family Historians" (www.dcn.davis.ca.us/~vctinney/archives.htm). This site includes links to many different types of material and is also international in scope. It includes a link to the UNESCO (United Nations Education, Scientific and Cultural Organization) Archives Portal (www.unesco.org/webworld/portal_archives/) that can be used to locate and search archives and library collections worldwide.

The Library of Congress Web site (www.loc.gov/) is the source of online materials, information, and access to their catalogs. Specifically, the Local History and Genealogy Reading Room Web site (www.loc.gov/rr/genealogy/) provides a gracious plenty for genealogical researchers. The American Memory Project (http://memory.loc.gov/) archives grow daily with historical documents of all sorts and media that may be helpful to genealogical researchers. Another resource made available by the Library of Congress in cooperation with other cataloging organizations is the National Union Catalog of Manuscript Collections (www.loc.gov/coll/nucmc/). From this page, the researcher will find links to other resources including the Archival and Manuscript Repositories in the United States (http://lcweb.loc.gov/coll/nucmc/other.html). This Web site compiles links to archives by state. Remember the example search for Gilbert P. Finch in the Connecticut 1830 or 1840 Census discussed above? If I decide to travel to Connecticut to view the records, I can verify a holding library or archive and find out their policies, hours, etc. before traveling. Using the Archival and Manuscript Repositories site, I search Connecticut and find the Connecticut State Archives and the Connecticut Historical Society, connect to their sites and find the Connecticut Historical Society does not seem to have those census records. It appears that the Connecticut State Archives do have the Connecticut Census microforms, but I'll need to call or write them to verify they have them for 1830 and 1840.

The National Society Daughters of the American Revolution Library (http://dar.library.net) catalog is online and searchable. This is one of the most important genealogical and historical collections. The holdings are not confined only to materials related to the American Revolution. They cover the entire scope of United States history:

> "The DAR Library was founded in 1896 as a collection of genealogical and historical publications for the use of staff genealogists verifying application papers for the National Society Daughters of the American Revolution. Shortly after 1900 the growing collection was opened to the public and has remained so ever since. Non-members—of the Daughters of the American Revolution, the Sons of the American Revolution, or the Sons of the Revolution or the Children of the American Revolution—pay a small daily user fee to help maintain and to expand the Library's collections. The Library is one of the nation's premier genealogical research centers and was recently (1998) ranked the third most important of national institutions based on the uniqueness of sources in a listing by publisher Heritage Quest. In late 1998, the Library's book collection numbered some 150,000 volumes, the cataloging records for which constitute this catalog. Approximately 5,000 new titles enter the Library in any given year" (Daughters of the American Revolution, 2001).

The Newberry Library (www.newberry.org) has been described as "The jewel in the crown of genealogical research libraries in the United States." The library Web site has search guides for genealogical research that is supported by the Newberry's collection. The scope is multi-ethnic and international.

The Allen County Public Library (ACPL) (www.acpl.lib.in.us/genealogy/genealogy.html) is recognized by researchers as one of the best genealogical collections in the United States. Their genealogical collection rivals larger national libraries. The scope is multi-ethnic and international. The library Web site compiles, reviews, and links to recommended genealogical research Web sites.

The National Park Service Web site (www.nps.gov) links to and describes National Park Service managed museums, monuments, libraries, and archives available at those locations. Many of these sites have materials or exhibits that support genealogical research. Prominent among thousands of historical sites and other information accessible through the National Park Service site are:

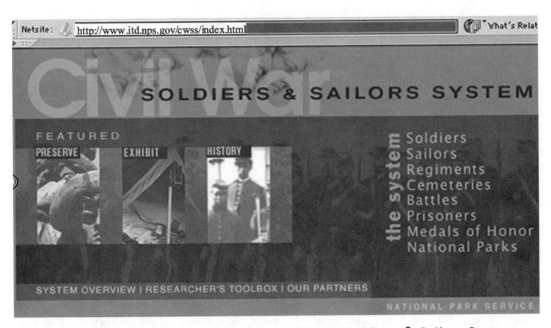

Netsite: http://www.itd.nps.gov/cwss/index.html

Figure 3.3. National Park Service Civil War Soldiers & Sailors System

- The "Civil War Soldiers and Sailors System" (www.itd.nps.gov/cwss/index.html) that has searchable databases of military records, battlefields, and national cemeteries for both the Union and Confederate forces. (Figure 3.3)
- The Statue of Liberty National Monument and Ellis Island National Monument Web site (www.nps.gov/elis/).

U.S. State Library Web sites can be invaluable sources of digitized genealogical data, collection information, and even a source for ordering copies of archival documents. The Wisconsin State Library's Bob Bocher (www.dpi.state.wi.us/dpi/dlcl/pld/statelib.html) has compiled a directory of state library Web sites.

For example, one of the first genealogy questions I answered as a reference librarian back in 1989 concerned materials held by the State Historical Society of Wisconsin Library. This library is one of the best in the United States in support of North American genealogical and historical research. While working with the patron to locate certain U.S. Civil War records, we came across a reference in an article to the State Historical Society of Wisconsin Library's collection of U.S. Civil War records. My patron and I telephoned and asked them about arrangements for someone to search for, retrieve, copy, and mail certain records. In the end, my patron traveled to Wisconsin to visit the library in person. Now, the State Historical Society of Wisconsin Library Web site (www.shsw.wisc.edu/genealogy/index.html) answers the questions we had in 1989 without a telephone call. Much of the collection is searchable through their catalog, some materials have been digitized, and some may be ordered online with a credit card.

The New York Public Libraries' The Irma and Paul Milstein Division of United States History, Local History and Genealogy (www.nypl.org/research/ chss/lhg/genea.html) is an outstanding collection with a Web site that describes the collection and everything the genealogical researcher needs to know to access it.

NARA National Archives and Records Administration

The NARA Web site is an essential source of information for any genealogical researcher looking for ancestors who came to the United States. The Genealogy page specifically www.nara.gov/genealogy links to tutorials, articles, and research guides for using some of the many records archived at NARA or the regional NARA depositories. Essential information includes descriptions of the contents and scope of the various U.S. census records, immigration related documents, military records, and other historical documents held by NARA. The fees required for microform rental, purchase, or document copies are published on the NARA Genealogy Page as well.

The researcher can also browse catalogs for the microformed collections of immigration records, census records, and many other historical collections. These catalogs can be used to identify the reel or fiche number of microformed information, and then order the appropriate microforms from NARA. The Web site provides e-mail addresses to use in ordering forms for ship passenger and arrival records, census records, military records, and other records. The NAIL (National Archives Information Locator) (www.nara.gov/nara/nail.html) search tool can be used to identify which NARA regional depositories or division of the main NARA location hold a given microfilm title and also whether a full-text transcribed or scanned image of a given NARA record is available.

"The NARA Archival Information Locator (NAIL) is a pilot database of selected holdings and is a working prototype for a future online catalog of holdings in Washington, DC, the regional archives, and the Presidential libraries" (National Archives and Records Administration, 2001).

NARA has begun scanning images of certain records and linking them through the NAIL database. The researcher may also elect to purchase or rent microformed documentation from commercial sources. Figures 3.4–3.9 are images of the NAIL Web page, Standards Search and an example search result with a digitized image from the "Rough Riders" collection of compiled military service records from the "Carded Records, Volunteer Organizations: Spanish-American War, 1898" series.

NARA tutorials, overviews and articles about genealogical research uses of the census and other records are an important resource on this site.

The microfilmed holdings of NARA also included census enumeration dis-

Location: http://www.nara.gov/nara/nail.html

NARA Archival Information Locator (NAIL)

A Prototype Database of Selected Holdings

Search for   **Search for**
Archival Holdings   **Microfilm Publications**

NAIL is the **working prototype** for a future online catalog of holdings in Washington, DC, the regional records services facilities, and the Presidential libraries. Until a full catalog is developed, NAIL will continue to serve as the NARA's on-line information system.

NAIL contains information about a wide variety of NARA's holdings across the country. Although NAIL contains more than **3,000** microfilm publications descriptions, **607,000** archival holdings descriptions, and **124,000** digital copies, it represents only a **limited portion** of NARA's vast holdings. To ensure you find all information in which you are interested, consult our home page or contact our reference staff.

Please note: not all images on the NARA web site are described in NAIL. You may also want to visit the Digital Classroom, the Online Exhibit Hall, and the individual Presidential Libraries' Web sites.

Please send comments and suggestions on the prototype to nail.mailbox@arch2.nara.gov

NAIL is updated every weekend.

Search for   **Search for**
Archival Holdings   **Microfilm Publications**

Figure 3.4.   NARA Archival Information Locator (NAIL)

NARA Archival Information Locator (NAIL)

Search for Archival Holdings

NAIL Standard Search

Basic search form which allows you to search for archival descriptions via keyword, media type, and/or NARA unit.

NAIL Expert Search

Advanced search form which allows you to search for archival descriptions via keyword, title, media type, NARA unit, description level, control number, and/or specific description level identifiers.

NAIL Digital Copies Search

Basic search form which searches only for archival descriptions that link to digital copies. Searches may also be limited by keyword, media type, and/or NARA unit.

NAIL Physical Holdings Search

Basic search form which allows you to search the physical holdings information for motion picture films and sound and video recordings of NARA's Motion Picture, Sound and Video Branch. Searches may be limited by media type, specific titles or title keywords, control number, and/or specific description level identifiers.

You may also want to search for descriptions of Microfilm Publications.

Please send comments and suggestions to nail.mailbox@arch2.nara.gov.

Figure 3.5.   NAIL Search Choices

trict maps. These are invaluable for searching census image files for urban areas, either online or browsing microfilmed copies. For example, in beginning to search census records for the family of Patrick E. Regan of Toledo, Ohio, we came up against the problem of where exactly in Toledo to find the

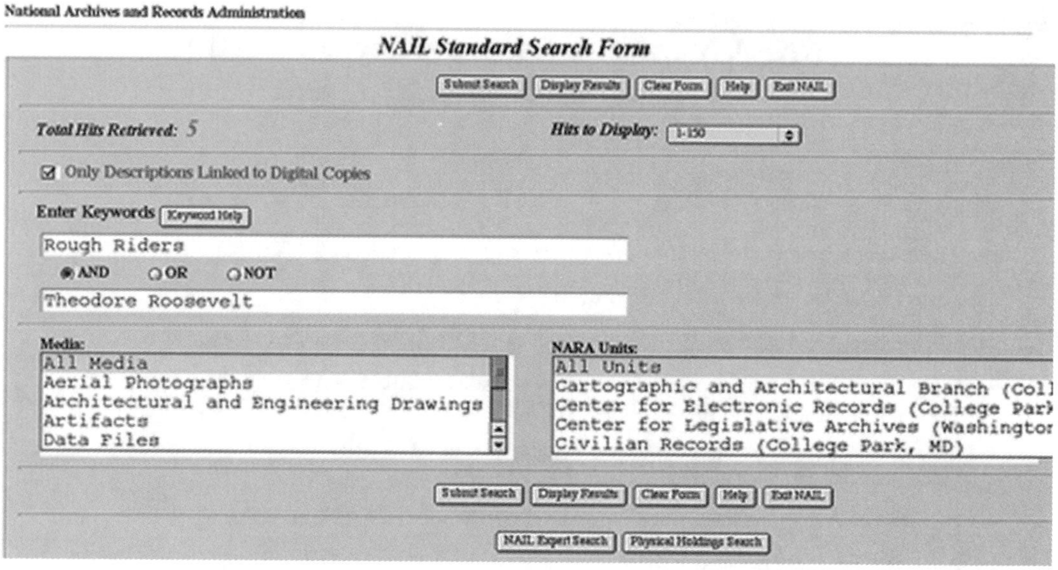

National Archives and Records Administration

Figure 3.6.   NAIL Standard Search Form

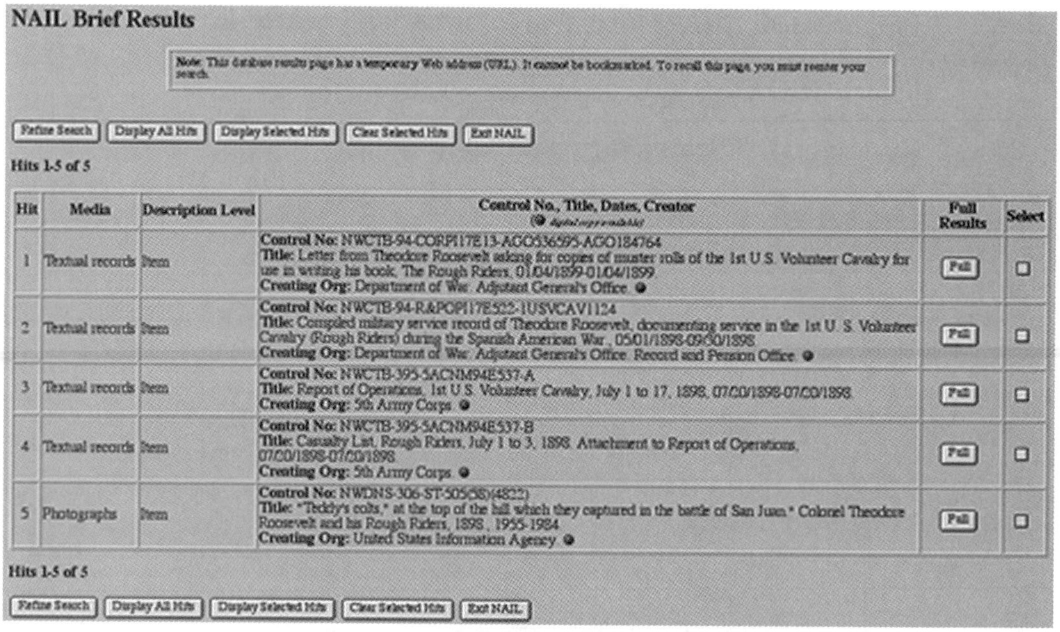

Figure 3.7.   NAIL Brief Results Display

family. The Patrick E. Regan family can be documented residents of Toledo from at least 1894 when the son William was born. In the online index and on the transcription page for the 1910 Ohio Census Miracode searched through Ancestry.com the family is discovered in census enumeration district 072. Attempts to find that family in the 1900 Census in that same enumeration district failed. The next step is to obtain census enumeration district maps for

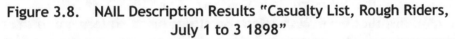

NAIL Full Results

How to Order

[Change Full Results Format] [Brief Results] [Refine Search] [Exit NAIL]

Control Number NWCTB-395-5ACNM94E537-B
Media Textual records
Descr. Level Item
Record Group 395
Series 5ACNM94E537
Item B
Title Casualty List, Rough Riders, July 1 to 3, 1898. Attachment to Report of Operations
Coverage Dates 07/00/1898-07/00/1898
Digital Copies ⊕ Thumbnails of online copies (with links to larger access files)
Creating Org. 5th Army Corps
Record Type/Genre lists
Scope & Content This is a list of the killed and wounded from the 1st U.S. Volunteer Cavalry (**Rough Riders**) at the Battle of San Juan Hill
General Note For additional information on the **Rough Riders**, see AGO Doc File 536595 and other War Department Records.
Variant Control# NWDT1-395-5AC-NM94E537-B
Contributors writer, Roosevelt, Theodore
See Also Series Description
Subject Ref. Spanish-American War
Access Unrestricted
Use Restrictions None
Items 1 item(s)
Contact Old Military and Civil Records (NWCTB), National Archives Building, 7th and Pennsylvania Avenue, NW, Washington, DC 20408 PHONE: 202-501-5385 FAX: 202-208-1903

Figure 3.8. NAIL Description Results "Casualty List, Rough Riders, July 1 to 3 1898"

[Previous Page] [Exit NAIL]

Casualty List, Rough Riders, July 1 to 3, 1898. Attachment to Report of Operations. PAGE1. (NWCTB-395-5ACNM94E537-B)

Figure 3.9. NAIL Scanned Image "Casualty List, Rough Riders, July 1 to 3 1898" First Page

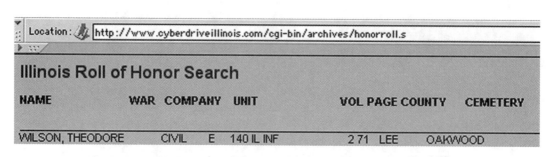

Figure 3.10.   1929 Illinois Roll of Honor Database

both 1910 and 1900 and compare them to identify where the family might be found. It may also be necessary to locate the family's street address during each year. NARA has been microfilming a collection of city directories that may prove valuable for this researcher.

Military record overviews and e-mail addresses to use in ordering forms to order copies of military service records are another important resource on the NARA Web site. For example, a researcher might perform a search for Civil War veterans in the MOA project Web site, The Civil War Soldiers and Sailors System, or other Civil War veterans listings on the Internet and then go to NARA to order the forms to use to order military record copies. In my own research I located my great-great-grandfather Theodore Wilson in the Database of Illinois 1929 Roll of Honor Search and the Illinois Civil War Veterans Database Search (www.cyberdriveillinois.com/departments/archives/databases.html). Figures 3.10 and 3.11 show the search results from both indexes. The Ancestry.com Civil War Pension Images also located a pension application from Theodore's widow Caroline. This image is shown in Figure 3.12. The data is very basic indeed. The NARA site describes the forms needed to be filed to obtain copies of any detailed records that might be available.

The NARA Web site is also the best place for the researcher to begin learning about U.S. immigration and naturalization records when they identify an immigrant ancestor. For example, in researching the Andres Palos family from Ohio to Texas and then to Mexico, the NARA Immigration Records overview (www.nara.gov/genealogy/immigration/immigrat.html) was used to discover when and what kind of data were collected from Mexican immigrants crossing the boarder into Texas. This example will be expanded on in Part 4.

Using Courthouses and Other Local Government Documents Archives

The Vital Records search site (www.vitalrec.com/) discussed in Part 2 is an ideal way to locate Web sites, physical addresses, and other contact information for courthouses and local government document archives. This database also describes what kinds and date ranges of records can be found at a given local government site. Given that information you can plan your correspon-

Illinois Civil War Veterans Database Search

Location: http://www.cyberdriveillinois.com/cgi-bin/archives/civilwar.s

NAME	RANK	COMPANY	UNIT	RESIDENCE
WILSON, THEODORE	REC	F	36 IL US INF	CHILI
WILSON, THEODORE	MUS	I	51 IL US INF	CANTON
WILSON, THEODORE	PVT	K	95 IL US INF	MANCHESTER
WILSON, THEODORE	WAG	D	140 IL US INF	PALMYRA
WILSON, THEODORE	PVT	E	132 IL US INF	CANTON
WILSON, THEODORE H	PVT	E	139 IL US INF	LANCASTER

Figure 3.11.   Illinois Civil War Veterans Database Search

Figure 3.12.   Civil War Pension Index Image (Ancestry.com)

dence with the location—online, telephone, or postal mail—or plan to travel to the site. You might even find that one of your living family members can be contacted and asked to visit the physical location to obtain copies of vital records or other documentation.

The Google Web search engine (www.google.com) is also a good tool to use in finding local government Web sites.

Using Cemeteries, Churches, and Other Religous Organizations

Cemeteries, churches, and other religious organizations can be a powerful source of genealogical data. USGenWeb has volunteers transcribing tombstone data and church records. Many of the resources available on the Web from these types of sources are available through the USGenWeb national, state, or county Web pages. There are also other Web sites that can help to locate cemeteries or churches all over the world. Some of these also link to transcription projects, but primarily these can be used to plan for genealogical offline correspondence or travel to the cemetery or church locations.

The Cemetery Junction Directory (http://daddezio.com/cemetery/index.html) is extraordinary. The Cemetery Junction Directory (Figure 3.13) provides browsing and searching of cemetery listings from all over the world. For example, most of my mother's family is buried in Oakwood Cemetery in Dixon, Illinois. Using the Cemetery Junction Directory, I clicked on "United States Cemeteries," selected Illinois, and then searched for Oakwood. The listing for Oakwood Cemetery in Dixon, Illinois provided an address only. There was also an Oakwood Cemetery in Oakwood, Illinois and there were tombstone transcriptions available online for that location. This site is maintained by the D'Addezio family and is also an award-winning Italian genealogy Web site.

The National Cemetery System Web site (www.va.gov/cemetery/index.htm), which is part of the Department of Veterans' Affairs, is full of information about burials in national cemeteries. The site provides information about how to search for specific burials. Their records do not contain any personal information on veterans, but can be used to locate where a veteran is buried. Tombstone information might be useful and this information may be used to confirm veteran status.

Church records may be another valuable resource for the genealogical researcher. For example, knowing that John and Rosina Schumm joined the Grace Evangelical Church in Dixon, Illinois in 1900, I might find other information about them in records of that church. A Web site called Beliefnet (www.beliefnet.org) is a directory of contact information for thousands of churches, temples, mosques, and other religious/spiritual organizations. Beliefnet can be used to locate the church and check if they have a Web site. The church Web site might have information about the records of the church

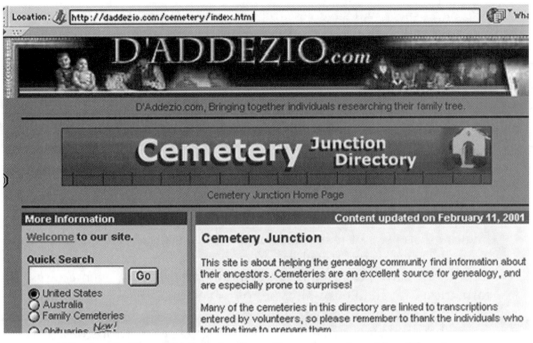

Figure 3.13.   D'Addezio.Com Cemetery Junction Directory

archives or at least contact information for requesting such records. At this time, it appears that there is only one evangelical church in Dixon, Illinois and that is Bethel Evangelical Church. They can be contacted by postal mail or telephone, to ask about what records they might have from the Grace Evangelical Church that might help in researching the John Schumm family.

Cyndi's List also has a comprehensive collection of religious organization Web sites that provide information related to genealogy research.

Travel Resources

The Internet assists the genealogical researcher in making travel plans in three ways:

1. Allows them to avoid travel altogether.
2. Allows them to plan where they will need to travel and dates and times for their visits.
3. Provides resources to use in identifying and booking economical transportation and lodging in locations all over the world.

The most valuable of these, in my opinion, is that the information provided, on or through Web sites, may allow researchers to avoid travel altogether. Researchers may find the materials they need are online transcribed or as scanned images, they may find that they can order copies of documentation online, over the telephone, or by postal correspondence.

103

The second aspect will save researchers time and problems when they do need to travel to locations holding materials that they need to access. Using Web sites as discussed above lets genealogical researchers plan their travel itinerary to take best advantage of their time. A related aspect is that using the information on these Web sites can take the burden off of librarians in explaining to patrons that they will need to travel and write to continue their research.

The third aspect is something the researchers themselves will need to decide to take advantage of. Some tools that have proven especially helpful are:

- Travelocity.com (www.travelocity.com/)
  Complete travel services available—car, plane, hotel, specials. This is the favorite travel site of many librarians.
- Yahoo! Travel (http://travel.yahoo.com/)
  Central air travel, car rental, hotel/motel reservations, even cruises. Information is available for all types of travelers.
- The Trip.com (www.thetrip.com/)
  Central air travel, car rental, and hotel/motel reservations designed for business travelers. Compare prices, too.

Exploring Special Genealogical Communications Topic: Adoptees and Birth Parent Searches

"If you are adopted, you have twice the opportunity to conduct research on your background. You are now a part of your adoptive family's history, and by learning more of this you may gain a stronger sense of belonging within this family. You may also be able to trace your biological family's roots, although this might prove to be quite a challenge. Legally, birth-parent records are sealed at least until the adoptee is 18 years of age. This was meant to be a mutually protective law, sensitive to all parties' needs . . . Adoptees make up 2 percent of the American population, and this proportion may continue to grow. Adoptees, once they are 18, have legal access to biological family records in most states. They can even sign up on adoption registers to be matched with their birth parents, if their birth parents have also registered" (Kavasch, 1996:29–30).

The National Adoption Information Clearinghouse (NAIC) Web site (www.calib.com/naic/) is a good starting place for anyone interested in locating birth parents or children placed for adoption, as well as for people looking for good information and support for adopting children. The NAIC, " . . . a comprehensive resource on all aspects of adoption, is a service of the Children's Bureau, Administration on Children, Youth and Families, Administration for Children and Families, Department of Health and Human Services" (National Adoption Information Clearinghouse, 2001).

The NAIC provides several fact sheets that either overview emotional and psychological issues critical in the birth parent/adopted child search process or facts related to access to information. For example: "Searching for Birth Relatives," "The Impact of Adoption on Birth Parents," "Resources for State Adoption Statutes," and "Access to Adoption Records." The latter two contain tables with the state codes and information about vital record access for all 50 states, Puerto Rico, the District of Columbia, and others. The NAICS publishes a printed list of Internet reunion and registry sites. Call (888) 251-0075. It is their policy to link only to other government sponsored or funded sites. To that end the NAIC Database "National Adoption Directory Online" links to the Web sites of state-supported or licensed agencies that provide registry or search support services for adoptees and birth families, as well as adoption support for individuals looking for children to adopt.

There are literally hundreds of Internet adoption search registries for both adoptees seeking their birth parents and birth parents seeking the children they placed for adoption. As with all Internet research tools, it is advisable to carefully read the privacy policies at any sites used. "Tina's Adoption Site" Web site (www.geocities.com/capitolhill/9606/) provides a compilation of international resources for adoption research including links to legal information and vital records access. This site is compiled and reviewed by Tina M. Musso (tmusso@usa.net). Her resume is linked from the page. Tina's "Adoption Registries and Forums" area contains listings and links to international registries and support organizations for adoptees and birth parents.

These registries can work when both parties wish to be found. For example, one of my students (name withheld on request) used Cyndi's List and found several registry sites for birth parents searching for the children they had placed for adoption. Through those registrations she networked and found the daughter she had given up for adoption 20 years ago. Her daughter had registered in hopes of finding her birth family. The great value of the Internet is people, people, people.

Putting Your Family History Information on the Web—GEDCOM Files

Family History Web pages are the most numerous genealogical sites on the Internet. Thousands of people put their family history data on Web pages to share with other researchers. Family History Web pages are also some of the most valuable forms of genealogical information on the Internet. They are the Web-published family histories and genealogies of fellow genealogical researchers. The useful aspect of these Web-published genealogies is that you can contact the person who compiled them and ask them to share their documentation and offer to share your genealogical data and documentation as well.

"The maiden name of my ancestor is on 1,000 Web sites, but does that mean it's true? Maybe yes, but maybe no. What is a researcher to do? If possible, begin a dialogue with the creator of the Web site or the submitter of the data. Some will respond and some will not; some will have obtained the information from someone else, and you'll start getting 'referrals.' If you ask for proof, you may find that they have it or you may find that they do not have it. There is a great deal of variation. Keep in mind, though, that this process doesn't mean the online sources should be ignored, for I have encountered plenty of print sources with no documentation and a compiler who was not really concerned about 'where' the information came from" (Neill, 2000).

All of the genealogical metasites discussed in Part 2 either provide a family history data upload and Web site storage service, or have links to sites that do. All of them have different registration requirements, unique procedures for uploading or inputting your data, as well as different privacy and access policies. The privacy and access policy issues can be tricky. Some sites literally sell access to search your genealogical information once you've uploaded it, or download the information to CD-ROM and publish it. Policies vary considerably. It is wise to read carefully all policy statements available on any site you consider using. If no policy statements on the privacy and use of the "free" family tree Web sites are available, then using such a site would be risky.

In publishing genealogies on the Web, we also must address a potential problem with information about living individuals. Most genealogical researchers agree that such information should be private, but you'll find information about living individuals as well on some sites. Information about birth dates and places of residence of living individuals can be used to check credit records and even to perpetrate identify theft.

There isn't really any "law" that governs this release of information, although all the genealogical organizations represented on RootsWeb strongly advise that any information about living individuals be provided online **only** with explicit permission from that living individual. For example, on the multi-family genealogy site "AllFam: Some American Families and their Origins" (http://homepages.rootsweb.com/~allfam/) living individuals are indicated with a note "(Details Withheld)." Ancestry.com displays living individuals as "Living Surname." The Ancestry.com family tree site automatically displays this for all entries without a death date in the appropriate field when it is searched. Only authorized users can see the full information for these living individuals.

The National Genealogical Society Web site (www.nsgenealogy.org) publishes "Guidelines for Publishing Web Pages on the Internet." This guideline is reproduced below with the permission of the National Genealogical Society:

"Guidelines For Publishing Web Pages On The Internet"

Recommended by the National Genealogical Society, May 2000

Appreciating that publishing information through Internet web sites and web pages shares many similarities with print publishing, considerate family historians—

- apply a single title to an entire web site, as they would to a book, placing it both in the <TITLE> HTML tag that appears at the top of the web browser window for each web page to be viewed, and also in the body of the web document, on the opening home, title or index page.
- explain the purposes and objectives of their web sites, placing the explanation near the top of the title page or including a link from that page to a special page about the reason for the site.
- display a footer at the bottom of each web page which contains the web site title, page title, author's name, author's contact information, date of last revision and a copyright statement.
- provide complete contact information, including at a minimum a name and e-mail address, and preferably some means for long-term contact, like a postal address.
- assist visitors by providing on each page navigational links that lead visitors to other important pages on the web site, or return them to the home page.
- adhere to the NGS "Standards for Sharing Information with Others" regarding copyright, attribution, privacy, and the sharing of sensitive information.
- include unambiguous source citations for the research data provided on the site, and if not complete descriptions, offering full citations upon request.
- label photographic and scanned images within the graphic itself, with fuller explanation if required in text adjacent to the graphic.
- identify transcribed, extracted or abstracted data as such, and provide appropriate source citations.
- include identifying dates and locations when providing information about specific surnames or individuals.
- respect the rights of others who do not wish information about themselves to be published, referenced or linked on a web site.
- provide web site access to all potential visitors by avoiding enhanced technical capabilities that may not be available to all users, remembering that not all computers are created equal.
- avoid using features that distract from the productive use of the web

site, like ones that reduce legibility, strain the eyes, dazzle the vision, or otherwise detract from the visitor's ability to easily read, study, comprehend or print the online publication.

- maintain their online publications at frequent intervals, changing the content to keep the information current, the links valid, and the web site in good working order.
- preserve and archive for future researchers their online publications and communications that have lasting value, using both electronic and paper duplication.

©2000 by National Genealogical Society. Permission is granted to copy or publish this material provided it is reproduced in its entirety, including this notice.

Committees § Standards (www.ngsgenealogy.org/comstandweb.htm).

RootsWeb provides a detailed help area for information about sharing your genealogical data on the Web. This is located at http://helpdesk.rootsweb.com/FAQ/wcindex.html. This site includes technical support information, as well as details about protecting the privacy of living individuals when publishing genealogical data on the Internet. RootsWeb's The WorldConnect project (http://worldconnect.rootsweb.com/) is a set of tools that allow users to upload, modify, link, and display their family trees as a means to share their work with other researchers.

Technically, the main requirement for uploading your data to these Web sites is that you have your genealogy information stored or converted to a standard genealogical database format called GEDCOM. GEDCOM is the standard computer format for genealogical data.

Most genealogical database software will export and import data in the GEDCOM format. For example, the Reunion software (Mac OS) will output to either GEDCOM or text and import GEDCOM, text (tab or return delimited data from spreadsheet or database software, etc.), or another database created with the Reunion software. GEDCOM format standardization allows genealogical data to be imported into genealogical database software without having to retype the information.

Some free family tree Web site storage services will also allow you to type all the information into their site directly. For example, my dad-in-law put the Kovacs/Kacsandy genealogical data into the Online Family Tree area of Ancestry.com and set up access for all of the interested family members. Initially, he had put the data into an Excel spreadsheet, so he retyped all of the data into the Online Family Tree Web site that he created for the Kovacs/Kacsandy family. I logged onto the Kovacs/Kacsandy area with my assigned username and set up a password. I used the Online Family Tree option to download all of the data my dad-in-law had typed in as a GEDCOM file. Downloading the data as a GEDCOM file was a matter of clicking on the document with the down arrow icon and directing the computer where to store the file. I started up my own Reunion software and imported the file. I now have my own local copy of all the work done by my dad-in-law on the Kovacs/Kacsandy genealogy to continue my own work.

There are many good commercial genealogical database packages that will save GEDCOM files for uploading to the Internet. The Genealogy Software Springboard site (www.gensoftsb.com/) lists and reviews hundreds of genealogy database software programs. Genealogy Software Springboard is a searchable database of genealogical freeware, shareware, and commercial products. Downloadable software is screened for viruses and other problems and also described and rated. The Genealogy Software Springboard site also has a good tutorial on GEDCOM files.

The Internet provides tools and resources for locating and communicating with living family members and fellow genealogical researchers. It is up to the individual researcher to establish proper and effective communications for themselves. Many libraries, archives, churches, courthouses, and other local government entities that are recognized sources of genealogical information and documentation have a presence on the Internet. The Web sites of these organizations can be used to verify the existence and location of genealogical documentation, to plan correspondence, or travel to these locations to obtain documentation. An increasing number of these Web sites are providing scanned images or transcriptions of their locally held genealogical documents and records.

References

Daughters of the American Revolution. 2001. [Online]. Available: http://dar.library.net/ [2001, October 23].

Federation of Genealogical Societies. 2001. [Online]. Available: www.fgs.org [2001, September 5].

Kavasch, E.B. 1996. *A Student's Guide to Native American Genealogy*. Phoenix, Ariz.: Oryx Press.

Landrum, G. 1992. *The Famous DAR Murder Mystery*. New York: St. Martin's Press.

Making of America. 2001. [Online]. Available: http://moa.umdl.umich.edu/ [2001, October 23].

National Adoption Information Clearinghouse. 2001. [Online]. Available: www.calib.com/naic [2001, October 23].

National Archives and Records Administration. 2001. [Online]. Available: www.nara.gov/nara/nail/nailgen.html [2001, October 23].

Neill, M.J. 2000. "It's on 1,000 Web Sites." *Ancestory Daily News* [Online]. Available: www.ancestory.com/library/view/news/articles/3203.asp [2001, October 23].

University of Idaho Library Special Collections. 2001. [Online]. Available: www.uidaho.edu/special-collections/other.repositories.html [2001, October 23].

Activity 3.1. Interviewing The Family

Overview:

In this activity you will use the basic questions from Part 1 Activity 1.2 to develop a questionnaire for interviewing family members about what they know about the family.

STEP 1.	Decide who you will interview. Mother? Father? Grandfather(s) or grandmother(s)? Aunt(s) or uncle(s)? Siblings?
STEP 2.	How will you contact the people you will interview? In-person? Telephone? Postal mail? E-mail?
STEP 3.	What limitations can you think of in terms of memory, health, and attention span will the people interviewed potentially experience? (For example, if your grandmother may have Alzheimer's, how will that affect her answers to your questions? If your mother is usually busy interacting with her grandchildren, will she have difficulty concentrating on your questions or finding time to answer them? Your father thinks that all this genealogy stuff is garbage—how will that affect his answers if he does answer?)
STEP 4.	Carefully record the person interviewed's name, date of birth, the date of the interview, their relationship with you, and other details that you think might be important. Write this information down on paper or type it into a computer document or database.
STEP 5.	Using the questions you answered, as well as those you were unable to answer in Part 1 Activity 1.2, ask your family members for verification of the answers you knew and their answers to the questions you were unable to answer.

- If you do this in-person record their answers by taking notes or by using a recorder (ask their permission to record).
- If you do this on the telephone, record their answers by taking notes or using a phone recorder device (ask their permission to record).
- If you do the interview in a letter sent postal mail, hopefully the written answers will be returned to you in postal mail.
- If you do the interview through e-mail, hopefully the written answers in electronic form will be returned to you in e-mail.

Note: If you are working self-paced and would like instructor feedback e-mail your responses and questions to *diane@kovacs.com*

Activity 3.2.   Finding Family Members and/or Fellow Genealogical Researchers

Overview:

In this activity you will use the RootsWeb (www.rootsweb.com/) site to identify appropriate genealogical discussion lists (called mailing lists on RootsWeb) and bulletin boards hosted or listed by RootsWeb. Then you will visit the Society Hall to browse and locate contact information for genealogical and historical organizations including those with Web sites (www.familyhistory. com/societyhall).

STEP 1.	Use your Web browser to connect to RootsWeb http://www.rootsweb.com/. Read through the page looking for "Mailings Lists" and "Message Boards."
STEP 2.	First click on the "Mailing Lists" link. How many mailing lists does RootsWeb list here? Scroll down through this page and scan all the different types of mailing lists that are available.
STEP 3.	Near the bottom of the screen click on the link for "Heraldry." Click through on the link for the "Heraldry" mailing list. Read through the description. Note the instructions for subscribing and unsubscribing. You may also wish to search the archives. Is this a discussion you'd be interested in joining?
STEP 4.	Go back to the main RootsWeb page and click on a link for a mailing list that interests you (e.g., Surnames, etc.). Which mailing list or lists interested you? Did you go ahead and subscribe?
STEP 5.	Go back to the main RootsWeb page and click on the "Message Boards" link. Read through the options on this page.
STEP 6.	Use the "BoardFinder" search tool to locate a message board for the surname "Smith." Scan through the messages. What kinds of questions do people ask? Note the options for posting your own questions, subscribing to the message boards, and searching the archives of the message boards "Genconnect."
STEP 7.	Go back to the Message Boards page and Use the "BoardFinder" search tool to locate a message board in an area that interests you. What did you look for? (Surname? State? Country? County?)
STEP 8.	Use your Web browser to connect to the Society Hall http://www.familyhistory.com/societyhall/
STEP 9.	Click on the link "Search for information about societies." Scroll

down and enter a search for "National Genealogical Society." Click through on the link for "National Genealogical Society." Read through the description. Is this an organization that interests you?

STEP 10.   Go back to the Search page and look for a genealogical organization of your choice. What did you search for? (e.g., keyword, state, city, etc.) Did you find a group that interests you?

Note: If you are working self-paced and would like instructor feedback e-mail your responses and questions to *diane@kovacs.com*

Activity 3.3. Learning from the National Archives and Records Administration (NARA) Genealogy Page and the NARA Archival Information Locator (NAIL)

Overview:

The NARA site has great potential and real information value:

- The growing collection of digitized records.
- The catalogs/indexes to the microformed collections (immigration lists, Freedman's information (African American records), and other really valuable information that you can use to identify the reel or fiche number of microformed information and then borrow them from NARA regional libraries or even purchase or rent microforms for your library).
- Tutorials and articles on genealogical, historical, or other research topics.

The best part of the NARA site is that you can see what NARA has in terms of collections, browse microform catalogs, request forms, and find out how to submit document orders, and also go to the regional NARA locations and get assistance and materials. The NARA site sometimes changes layout and so can be difficult to navigate. Stay flexible and read the Web pages for clues.

In this activity you will also use the "NARA Archival Information Locator" or NAIL Search tool.

STEP 1.   Use your Web browser to connect to http://www.nara.gov/genealogy
           Read completely through the information on this page.

STEP 2.   Click on the link for "Genealogical and Biographical Resources." Read through the information provided. The direct URL is http://www.nara.gov/publications/microfilm/biographical/genbio.html.
           When you have finished reading click back to the main NARA Genealogy page. Click through on any links that interest you.

STEP 3.   When you have finished scanning the NARA genealogy page contents, click on the link for "NARA Archival Information Locator (NAIL)," read over the page. Then click on "Genealogical Data in Nail?." The direct URL is http://www.nara.gov/nara/nailfaq.html#q2.

STEP 4.   Read through the "Genealogical Data in Nail?" responses, then click on the link "Search Hints for Genealogical Data in NAIL" The direct URL is http://www.nara.gov/nara/nail/nailgen.html.

STEP 5.   Read through the "Search Hints for Genealogical Data in NAIL."
               This tutorial and overview is essential in using the NAIL tool
               for searching for digitized genealogical records or for micro-
               form catalog information.

STEP 6.   Locate and read the hints for searching NAIL for "description
               of the Kern-Clifton Roll of Cherokee Freedmen, January 16,
               1867."

STEP 7.   Click on "Search NAIL." Perform the search. Select a record
               for viewing.

STEP 8   Using the resources described in "Search Hints for Genealogical
               Data in NAIL" search for information in a collection of your
               choice. Did you retrieve any results? Were there digitized im-
               ages available with your results?

Note: If you are working self-paced and would like instructor feedback e-mail
your responses and questions to *diane@kovacs.com*

Activity 3.4. Researching with the Making of America Project—University of Michigan and Cornell University

Overview:

This activity focuses on the full-text searchable archives of the Making of America (MOA) Project. This is a guided exploration of some of the areas that may be useful for genealogical research with focus on the "Official Records of the War of the Rebellion" materials through the Cornell University Making of America project site.

STEP 1.	Use your Web browser to connect to the University of Michigan MOA project site http://moa.umdl.umich.edu. Read through the page.
STEP 2.	Click on the link "Go to MoA Books." Read through the contents. Which two titles interest you the most?
STEP 3.	Click back to the main University of Michigan MOA project page and click on the link "Go to MoA Journals." Read through the contents. Which two titles interest you the most?
STEP 4.	Use your Web browser to connect to the Cornell University MOA project site http://library5.library.cornell.edu/moa/. Read through the page.
STEP 5.	Click on Browse. Read through the contents. Click on the link for "The War of the Rebellion: a Compilation of the Official Records of the Union and Confederate Armies (1880 - 1901)."
STEP 6.	Use the "simple" search option to search on the keyword "Father." Click on the result "Series 1 - Volume 1 4 matches in 4 of 768 pages."
STEP 7.	Read through the page. Scroll down and click on the result "p. 158 1 match of 'father'."
STEP 8.	Read through the resultant screens. In what kind of document does the keyword 'father' occur? Would this document be useful for a genealogical researcher? Note: You will need to page forward to 159 to read the entire document.
STEP 9.	Use the search options to search on a name or other keyword of your choice. What did you find in the text of the records?

Note: If you are working self-paced and would like instructor feedback e-mail your responses and questions to *diane@kovacs.com*

Part 4

How to Locate International, African American, and Native American Ancestors; Heraldry and Lineage Societies

"Not that he had not made every effort to remain. But the rains had ruined his crop for the third consecutive year. Finally, he'd thrown up his hands, and to his mother said: "T'hell with it. I'll go to America."... The Tea Kettle whistled downstairs in Mrs. Slattery's kitchen and Danny woke up in the present. Could his grandfather have imagined that a grandson of his would come back to this same rocky shore, to dig among cemetery stones over-grown with mosses and ferns, searching for the names of his ancestors? Could he have ever understood that just as Daniel P. O'Flaherty had fled from this land to escape its damp and misty past, his grandchildren would come back through the mist with passenger lists, civil records, and data gleaned from old census reports, to recapture that very past?" (Harrington, 1995:40-41).

—

"He would go over the slave roster tomorrow. He was too sleepy tonight . . . It was long past midnight, and he was still bent over the records of births and deaths from 1800-1812 . . . He cast wide his research net, then slowly drew it toward him. Medley Orion, born around 1785, was reported to be a beautiful woman. Her extraordinary color was noted twice in the records; her lovely cast of features must have been delicious. White people rarely noted the physiognomy of black people unless it was to make fun of them. But an early note in a lady's hand . . . stated these qualities" (Brown, 1994:99-103).

The Ankh-Morpork Royal College of Heralds turned out to be a green gate in Mollymog Street. Vimes tugged on the bell-pull . . . Vimes watched through the window as he limped back to continue what he had been doing before Vimes's appearance . . . What he had been doing was setting up a living coat of arms . . . There was a large shield. Cabbages, actual cabbages, had been nailed to it . . . The little owl fluttered from its perch and landed on a large ankh that had been glued to the top of the shield. The two hippos flopped out of their pool and took up station on either side . . . The old man unfolded an easel in front of the scene, placed a canvas on it, picked up a palette and brush, and shouted, "Hup-la!" . . . The hippos reared rather arthritically. The owl spread its wings. "Good Gods," murmured Vimes. "I always thought they just made it up!" . . . "Made it up, sir? Made it up?" said a voice behind him. "We'd soon be in trouble if we made things up, oh dear me yes."

Vimes turned. Another little old man had appeared behind him, blinking happily through thick glasses . . . "I'm sorry I couldn't meet you at the gate but then we're very busy at the moment," he said, holding out his spare hand. "Croissant Rouge Pursuivant."

"Er . . . you're a small red breakfast roll?" said Vimes, nonplussed.

"No, no. no. It means Red Crescent. It's my title, you see. Very ancient title. I'm a Herald . . . " Red Crescent consulted his scroll. "Good. Good. How you feel about weasels?" he said.

"Weasels?"

"We have got some weasels, you see. I know if they're not *strictly* a heraldic animal, but we seem to have some on the strength and frankly I think I'm going to have to let them go unless we can persuade someone to adopt them, and that had upset Pardessus Chatain Pursuivant . . . "

"Pardessus . . . You mean the old man out there?" said a Vimes. "to I mean . . . why's he . . . I thought you . . . I mean the, a coat of arms is just a design. You don't have to paint it from life!"

Red Crescent looked shocked. "Well, I suppose if you want if you want to make a complete mockery of the whole thing, yes, you could just *make it up* . . . " (Pratchett, 1996:19-22).

In this part, we'll discuss using the Internet to continue genealogical research from the point at which the researcher discovers the existence of international ancestors. At this point the language, history, and culture of the country of origin becomes essential information. African American genealogical researchers will have the same kind of challenge when they trace ancestors back to pre-1862 in the United States. Similar challenges affect research of Native American ancestors. Heraldry and lineage societies that are special areas of genealogical interest are also addressed.

In order to do international, African American, or Native American genealogical research it is necessary to have a strong knowledge of history. It is actually very interesting to study history when part of the story involves your family. The political, legal, cultural, and social relationships between African American, Native American, and the government and other people of the U.S. have determined what kinds of records will be available to the researcher.

The topics covered in this part are advanced in comparison to the topics covered in the previous parts. In order to use the information discussed in this part, the researcher must have already researched their family to a point where they have documentation that an ancestor came from another country at some point, was an African American slave in the United States, or was a member of a Native American tribal group.

International Genealogical Research

Genealogical researchers who have established that an ancestor at some time moved from one country to another will need to begin researching internationally. The first question to ask in doing or assisting with international genealogical research is which country and which language is the research to be focused on. International genealogical researchers will need to know the history and the language of their ancestor's countries of origin.

Stepping back a bit, before the researcher begins looking for information in another country, they must first know where their ancestor came from. This is primarily a problem for researchers in North and South America. Everyone on these continents—who is not a Native American—has an immigrant ancestor. So nearly every North and South American genealogical researcher will eventually need to do research internationally. Researchers in these North and South American countries will need to know something about the history and patterns of immigration. For example, researchers in the United States will need to know something about the history and patterns of immigration in the United States relevant to the ethnicity and countries of origin of their ancestors. The history of immigration in the United States is very complex and multi-layered. A very brief overview of the history of immigration in the United States is that different ethnic groups—or groups of people from the same country or region—settled in different U.S. regions for many different reasons including economic, cultural, and political. For example, in the eastern United States people of the British Isles originally concentrated—and then spread slowly west. In the Cleveland/Pittsburgh/Detroit regions, the steel companies went to Hungary and other parts of Eastern Europe and actively recruited people to come here to work. In the far west you have many individuals of Spanish background, because California, Texas, Arizona, and other adjacent regions were settled by immigrants from Spain and Mexico.

At this writing, the Ellis Island Records represent the majority of full-text or scanned images of nineteenth- and twentieth-century naturalization and immigration records available through the Internet. As discussed in Part 3, there is plenty of good historical background information on the Internet. Early immigration records from the seventeenth and eighteenth centuries and early nineteenth century are sparse, although complete ships passenger lists online for early ships such as the Mayflower can be found on the Internet. Most of

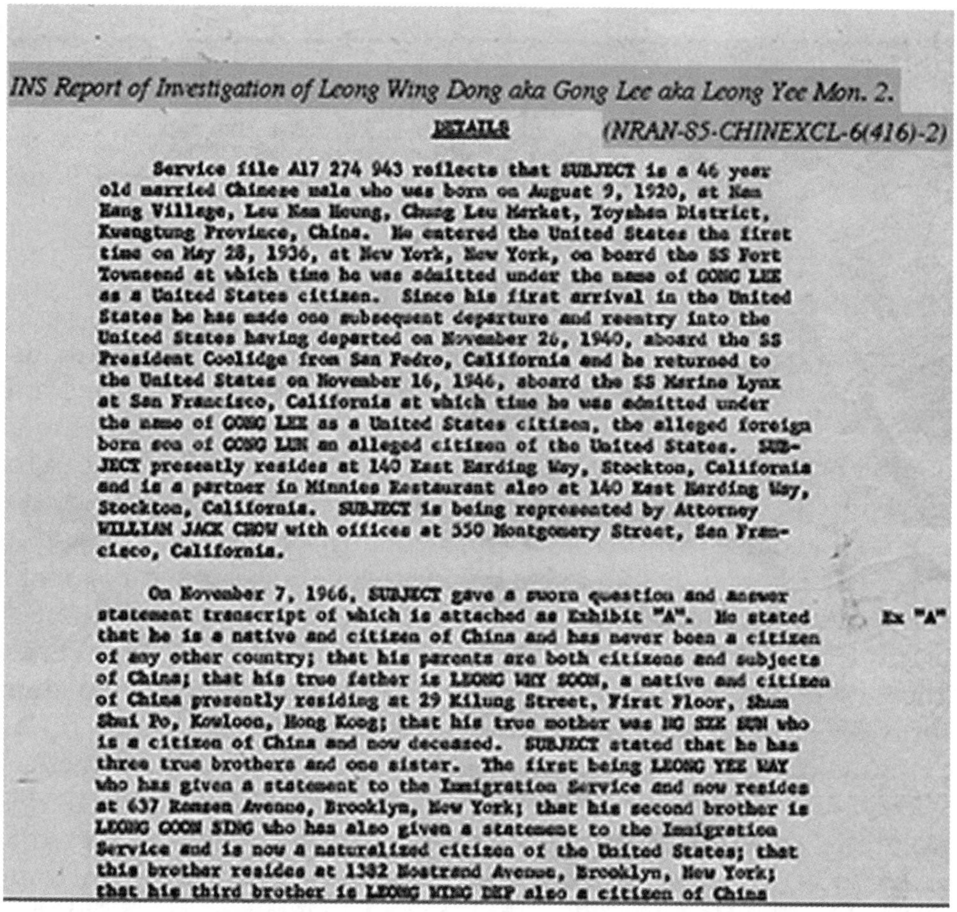

INS Report of Investigation of Leong Wing Dong aka Gong Lee aka Leong Yee Mon. 2.

DETAILS (NRAN-85-CHINEXCL-6(416)-2)

Service file A17 274 943 reflects that SUBJECT is a 46 year old married Chinese male who was born on August 9, 1920, at Nam Kang Village, Leu Kam Heung, Chung Leu Market, Toyshan District, Kwangtung Province, China. He entered the United States the first time on May 28, 1936, at New York, New York, on board the SS Fort Townsend at which time he was admitted under the name of GONG LEE as a United States citizen. Since his first arrival in the United States he has made one subsequent departure and reentry into the United States having departed on November 26, 1940, aboard the SS President Coolidge from San Pedro, California and he returned to the United States on November 16, 1946, aboard the SS Marine Lynx at San Francisco, California at which time he was admitted under the name of GONG LEE as a United States citizen, the alleged foreign born son of GONG LUN an alleged citizen of the United States. SUBJECT presently resides at 140 East Harding Way, Stockton, California and is a partner in Minnies Restaurant also at 140 East Harding Way, Stockton, California. SUBJECT is being represented by Attorney WILLIAM JACK CHOW with offices at 550 Montgomery Street, San Francisco, California.

On November 7, 1966, SUBJECT gave a sworn question and answer statement transcript of which is attached as Exhibit "A". He stated that he is a native and citizen of China and has never been a citizen of any other country; that his parents are both citizens and subjects of China; that his true father is LEONG WAY SOON, a native and citizen of China presently residing at 29 Kilung Street, First Floor, Shum Shui Po, Kowloon, Hong Kong; that his true mother was NG SEE SEN who is a citizen of China and now deceased. SUBJECT stated that he has three true brothers and one sister. The first being LEONG YEE WAY who has given a statement to the Immigration Service and now resides at 637 Remsen Avenue, Brooklyn, New York; that his second brother is LEONG COON SING who has also given a statement to the Immigration Service and is now a naturalized citizen of the United States; that this brother resides at 1382 Nostrand Avenue, Brooklyn, New York; that his third brother is LEONG MING DEP also a citizen of China

Ex "A"

Figure 4.1. NARA Image from "Chinese Exclusion Act" Series

these resources are databases of information contributed by genealogical researchers as they do their own research, so the coverage of names, dates, places, and times is scattered. Much information about individuals immigrating to regions within what has become the United States took place prior to any official government oversight. Many early records are found only in church, local historical archives, and personal papers. The RootsWeb U.S. Naturalizations search tool searches a collection of these resources. RootsWeb also hosts the Immigrant Ships Transcribers Guild (http://istg.rootsweb.com) that is the project of a group of volunteers to decipher and transcribe passenger lists as they do their own research. The passenger lists are the core feature of this Web site, but another valuable tool is "The Compass" page that links to tutorials, articles, and to specific areas on the NARA Web site with details about the different U.S. ports of entry and the records available for them. NARA has begun digitizing the records that it holds related to immigration and naturalization. The records that are available are searchable through the NARA Archival Information Locator (NAIL) that was discussed in Parts 2

Figure 4.2. Mexico WorldGenWeb Site

and 3. Figure 4.1 is a partial image from the NARA collection "Chinese Exclusion Acts," which is 409 case files.

The Immigration and Ships Passenger Lists Research Guide (http://home.att.net/~arnielang/shipgide.html) is a great tutorial for genealogical researchers wishing to locate and use passenger lists and other related kinds of records including naturalization and passport records.

The Immigration and Naturalization Service Web site (www.ins.usdoj.gov) provides a History, Genealogy, and Education page:

"This portion of the INS Web site contains information about the INS Historical Reference Library collection and services, documents concerning the history of the Service as well as of immigration law, procedure, and immigration stations, and instructions for historical and genealogical research using INS records" (Immigration and Naturalization Service, 2001).

Two example searches illustrate the typical information resources that the Internet can provide for researching ancestors who immigrated to the United States from other countries. The first example describes research using Mexican-U.S. immigration and naturalization information for the early twentieth century. The second example describes trying to locate German-U.S. immigration and naturalization information for the late nineteenth century.

I began research by interviewing my brother-in-law. I learned that his father Andres Palos was born in Needville, Texas in 25 Feb 1928. But Andres's father, Joseph Angelus Madera Palos, was born in Apozal, Zacatecas, Mexico on 19 Sep 1904. Beginning with the Mexico WorldGenWeb site (www.rootsweb.com/~mexwgw/) (Figure 4.2), we located some background information about obtaining vital records for the Zacatecas area via postal mail. Using the UsGenWeb Texas Web Fort Bend site's "Index to Cities & Towns in Texas" we located Needville, Texas in Fort Bend County. The next step will be to locate and search microfilmed records from Texas ports of entry from Mexico prior to 1928. As mentioned in Part 3, we learned from the

Dixon Evening Telegraph -DEATH NOTICE (penciled date 1940)

John Schumm

John Schumm, a resident of Dixon for 60 years, passed away this morning at 12:15 o'clock at his home 510 Squires avenue. He had been failing for the past five months. Mr. Schumm operated a tailor shop in Dixon for many years but retired some time ago.

He was born in Weitenburg, Germany, April 7, 1859 and came to this city in 1880 where he has since resided. Surviving him are his widow, five daughters and one son; Mrs. William Dunn of Stockton Calif., Mrs. Mary Prescott, Mrs. Anna Wilson, Mrs. Harriett Benson of this city, Mrs. Emma DeCamp of LaGrange and one son, Louis of Dixon. Funeral services will be held at Grace Evangelical church Wednesday afternoon at 2 o'clock, the pastor, The Rev. George Nielson officiating and with interment in Oakwood.

Figure 4.3. **Transcription of Newpaper Death Notice Clipping from** *Dixon Evening Telegraph* **for John Schumm**

NARA Web site overview "Mexican Border Crossing Records" (www.nara. gov/genealogy/immigration/mexican.html) that immigration records were not collected by the federal government until about 1906. In fact data was not collected at all for many immigrants who crossed the border regularly for work or to visit family.

The death notice clipping for my great-great-grandfather John Schumm (father of Ann Wilson) (Schumm) (Figure 4.3) states that he was born in Weitenburg, Germany on April 7, 1859 and arrived in Dixon, Illinois about 1880, and set up a tailor shop. First I searched the RootsWeb site for "John Schumm" and then just for "Schumm" and found no information relating to my John Schumm. I did find one message requesting information about his wife Rosina Schumm (Whorle), who according to her obituary (Figure 1.5 in Part 1 on page 19) came to the United States from Germany in 1880 as well. I sent the information that I possessed to the requesting individual via e-mail.

Historical knowledge is essential even if a researcher's ancestral country of origin and country of citizenship are the same. This is especially important for researchers working in countries that have had different forms of government in the past, or been under the control or jurisdiction of other countries. In doing Hungarian (Magyar) genealogical research, for example, it is important to know:

- the history of the original Magyar tribes,
- the Turkish invasion,
- the origins and extent of the Austro-Hungarian Empire,

- Hungarian participation in both World Wars,
- the partitioning of the Treaty of Trianon,
- the invasions of the Germans during World War II,
- the government controlled by the Communist party
- as well as the current democracy,
- and of course the exodus following the abortive anti-communist revolt of 1956.

Many countries offer illustrative examples. Europe and most countries of the Asian and African continents were at various times governed by many small regional or local governments or invaded and controlled or colonized by other nations. Egypt, for a specific example, was invaded and controlled by the Ptolemaic Greeks, Romans, French, Turkish, and British in turn, before regaining its independence in 1922.

The Internet is a good place to find the basic historical details, and very occasionally in-depth historical information. The World History Archives (www.hartford-hwp.com/archives/) is one such useful site. It is also profitable to use a Web search tool to search on the keyword History and the name of the country in which you are interested. Be careful that the sites listed provide information from authoritative sources. There is much "historical revision" on the Internet. By "historical revision" is meant the changing of historical facts or omitting of historical facts. For example, there are those that claim that the Holocaust—the murder of millions of Jews, Gypsies, and other people—by the Nazis didn't happen.

International genealogical research might also involve knowing the religious, political, or ethnic affiliations of your ancestors. Jewish people have ancestors from all over the world. The JewishGen.org Web site brings together many valuable Internet resources, powerful search tools, and best of all, people researching their Jewish ancestors and sharing their research. One of the most valuable features of the JewishGen.org site is in the JewishGen Databases section. ShtetlSeeker is a tool for helping researchers to identify place names in Russia and Eastern Europe that have undergone name changes or simply don't exist in modern times.

"Gypsy," "Rom," "Romany," and other "Traveler" ancestors may also be found in any part of the world. Cyndi's List provides some of the best sites for researching these ancestors under the category "Unique People's" (www.CyndisList.com/peoples.htm). These are just two of the many examples of religious or ethnic affiliations that affect international genealogical research.

Knowledge of historical geography is a critical genealogical research requirement. In researching Hungarian ancestors, for example, the researcher needs maps showing the various districts, cities, villages, and local governmental units over time. The WorldGenWeb project (http://worldgenweb.org) sites frequently provide high-quality historical maps.

Another requirement for doing international research is language. The researcher needs to either have reading knowledge of the language of the country of interest or have access to a reliable translator. This can be especially challenging if the language used in vital records is an archaic form. Two sites may be helpful in translating. Altavista's Babel Fish translation tool (http://world.altavista.com/) will perform a machine translation of several paragraphs at once from English to Spanish, French, German, Italian, Portuguese, Japanese, Korean, Chinese, or from these languages into English. Babel Fish will also translate Russian to English. A better solution is to hire a human translator or find a willing volunteer. RootsWeb's "Random Acts of Genealogical Kindness" project (http://raogk.rootsweb.com/) and the Genealogy Helplist project (www.helplist.org) are two volunteer groups where volunteer translators may be located. The WorldGenWeb project (http://worldgenweb.org) individual country pages may also offer translation services for fee or volunteer.

Cyndi's List (www.cyndislist.com) is an outstanding source for finding international genealogical research Web sites. Use the category list to choose the country, region, ethnic, or religious group of interest to find at least one good Web site for sub-categories. There are also extensive listings for the United Kingdom, Ireland, and Canada sub-categories. There are sub-categories for some specific regions and countries on the African continent. At this writing, Cyndi's List does not have a specific sub-category for Hungary, but there are several excellent and essential sites for Hungarian genealogical research listed under the "Austro-Hungarian Empire." Hungary does appear in the listings for the Federation of East European Family History Societies. There is a sub-category "Eastern Europe."

RootsWeb (www.rootsweb.org) hosts the WorldGenWeb projects, as well as the FreeBMD and FreeREG projects for United Kingdom researchers. The WorldGenWeb project (Figure 4.4) coordinates volunteers all over the world in various genealogically related projects. The WorldGenWeb Web site (http://worldgenweb.org/) also provides a metasite for international genealogical resources organized alphabetically by country, as well as by region and continent.

Everton's Genealogical Helper: International Genealogy Resources page (http://everton.com/reference/world-resource.php) is an excellent collection of international genealogical Web sites. This is an Internet publication of the well-known genealogical magazine. There are special features available only in the online edition, some research pointers, and links to other online resources. The international resource area is arranged by country name only, so it's easy to access. On the other hand, the Everton's international resource collection does not include a link for Mexico or any other Central or South American countries. Cyndi's List has a category "Hispanic, Central & South America, & the West Indies" that does include genealogical Web sites for Jamaica and many other countries.

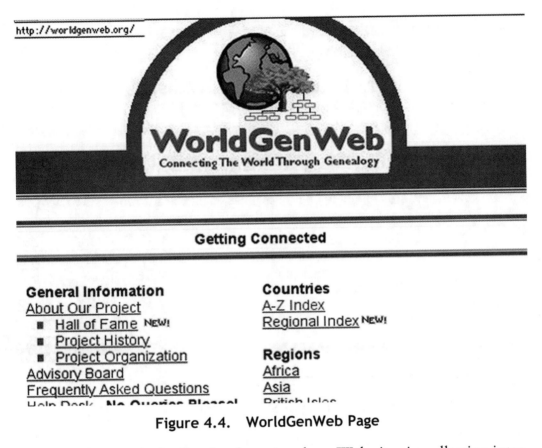

Figure 4.4. WorldGenWeb Page

There is also much duplication between these Web sites in collecting international genealogical resources, but all three metasites will be useful for the international genealogical researcher.

Using a general Web search engine can be frustrating and overwhelming because it may return too many sites and they will be of varying quality. For specific international genealogical searches, using a general Web search engine is an efficient way of locating Web sites. Google (www.google.com) is recommended because it has a good search result algorithm that tends to sort useful sites to the top of the search results list. For a simple search on the country name and "genealogy" or "genealogical" (e.g., "Hungarian genealogy") Google will usually retrieve many useful Web sites displayed on the first page of search results. Google has proved invaluable in locating Web sites to support the author's husband's Hungarian genealogical research.

Other good International genealogical resource collections include:

The LDS Church FamilySearch.org (www.familysearch.org) contains indexing for many international vital record collections as discussed in Part 2.

Morton Grove, Illinois Public Library's Webrary Collection (www.webrary.org/ref/genealogy.html) that has selected and annotated some of the best sites for European genealogical research

Location: http://www.ipl.org/ref/timeline/
the Internet Public Library

Slavery and Religion in America: A Time Line 1440-1866

1440's Portuguese begin to capture Africans off the coast of Mauritania and the Sengambia region.

1619 First Africans are brought to English colonies, in particular to Jamestown, Virginia.

Section from *Slave Caravan* as the image appeares in the English Abolitionist periodical, *The Anti Slavery Reporter and Aborigines Friend*, Series IV No. 1-2, 1881-1882.

Full Image (77 KB)

Figure 4.5.   Beginning of Slavery Time Line 1440-1866

African American Genealogical Research

Genealogical research for African Americans follows the same basic pattern as for any American ethnic group until the researcher reaches the era of slavery in the United States. Knowledge of this historical timeline is critical. Researchers looking for African American ancestors will need to know details about the history of slavery in Africa, the United States, as well as the rest of the world. They must also be aware of the legal relationships and key dates in the history of the legal relationships between the United States government and African American individuals (legal relationships such as when and where African Americans were considered people as opposed to merchandise and when and where they were treated legally as citizens of the United States). Carrie Bickner has published "Slavery and Religion in America: A Time Line 1440-1866" www.ipl.org/ref/timeline/ (1998). This is a detailed and thorough timeline with dates (Figure 4.5) and events relevant to both slavery and abolition with reference to international as well as U.S. events. It is published on the Internet Public Library Web site (www.ipl.org).

In *Black Roots: A Beginners Guide to Tracing the African American Family Tree* (2000), Tony Burroughs identifies six phases of African American Genealogy:

1. Gather Oral History and Family Records
2. Research the Family to 1870
3. Identify the Last Slave Owner
4. Research the Slave Owner and Slavery
5. Go Back to Africa
6. Research Canada and the Caribbean

Some African American genealogy researchers will not get to Step 3. Some few African American families do not have ancestors who were slaves in the United States. The researcher might find that their family came to the United States through the Caribbean nations, Mexico, or through Canada. At this point, their research becomes international. Some African Americans will even find that their ancestors were not slaves at any time in history.

A terrible tragedy in searching for slave ancestors is the failure of slavers and slave owners to record the names or origins of their "merchandise." The break up of families when slaves born in the United States were sold frequently, interrupted any slave family's attempts to keep records of births, deaths, and origins. Slave owners also tried to keep the people they owned ignorant and illiterate. Because of these factors, much slave ancestor research relies on knowing the family name and history of the slave owner.

Identifying a slave owner should reveal to the researcher which state the slave owner resided in. This information may be found in letters of emancipation, family correspondence, diaries, or recorded narratives. Recorded narratives based on interviews with former slaves may be a very helpful source for the genealogical researcher. The available narratives are rapidly being published on the Internet in the American Memory Project Collection "Born in Slavery: Slave Narratives from the Federal Writers' Project, 1936-1938" (http://memory.loc.gov/ammem/snhtml/snhome.html). Figure 4.6 is the image of one page of an interview with John Eubanks in which details of his birth, slavery, naming, experiences in the Union army, and subsequent marriage and family are recorded. Another good source is "American Slave Narratives: An Online Anthology" (http://xroads.virginia.edu/~hyper/wpa/wpahome.html).

Many slave-era records and other documents relating to the legal status of African Americans are archived in state and historical society libraries and archives. Slavery was a reality in almost every state to some extent before 1863. Even "Free" states frequently returned runaway slaves or were visited by slave owners from other states traveling with slaves. Records of slavery include:

- Bills of sale and receipts
- Letters of emancipation
- Divorce settlement documents
- Marriage contracts

Archie Koritz, Field Worker
Federal Writers' Project
Lake County - District #1   68
Gary, Indiana

EX-SLAVES

John Eubanks & Family

Gary's only surviving Civil War veteran was born a slave in Barren County, Kentucky, June 6, 1836.   His father was a mulatto and a free negro.   His mother was a slave on the Everrett plantation and his grandparents were full-blooded African negroes.   As a child he began work as soon as possible and was put to work hoeing and picking cotton and any other odd jobs that would keep him busy.   He was one of a family of several children, and is the sole survivor, a brother living in Indianapolis, having died there in 1935.

Following the custom of the south, when the children of the Everrett family grew up, they married and slaves were given them for wedding presents.   John was given to a daughter who married a man of the name of Eubanks, hence his name, John Eubanks.   John was one of the more fortunate slaves in that his mistress and master were kind and they were in a state divided on the question of slavery.   They favored the north.   The rest of the children were given to other members of the Everrett family upon their marriage or sold down the river and never saw one another until after the close of the Civil War.

Shortly after the beginning of the Civil War, when the north seemed to be losing, someone conceived the idea of forming negro regiments and as an inducement to the slaves, they offered them freedom if they would join the Union forces.   John's mistress and master told him that if he wished to join the Union forces, he had their consent and would not have to run away like other slaves were

Figure 4.6.   Interview with John Eubanks, American Memory Project Collection "Born in Slavery: Slave Narratives from the Federal Writers' Project, 1936-1938"

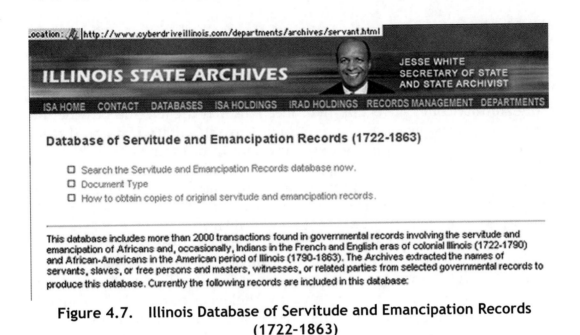

Figure 4.7.   Illinois Database of Servitude and Emancipation Records (1722-1863)

- Records of gifts (e.g., slaves given as birthday or wedding gifts)
- Leases
- Registration of transportation (e.g., some states and territories required the registration of slaves entering their domains)
- Records of runaway slaves
- Wills
- Household correspondence (e.g., letters, shopping lists, laundry instructions, farm production records, and other primary but not necessarily official documents).
- Diaries

There may be other documents that will be valuable, that don't fit into these categories.

Some state or historical society archives have published listings or catalogs of their holdings related to African American genealogical research in the slave era on the Internet. Some few have made searchable indexes of their holdings available on the Internet.

The Illinois State Archives (www.cyberdriveillinois.com/departments/archives/servant.html), for example, has published the "Database of Servitude and Emancipation Records (1722-1863)" (Figure 4.7).

"This database includes more than 2000 transactions found in governmental records involving the servitude and emancipation of Africans and, occasionally, Indians in the French and English eras of colonial Illinois (1722-1790) and African Americans in the American period of Illinois (1790-1863). The Archives extracted the names of servants, slaves, or free persons and masters, witnesses, or related parties from selected governmental records to produce this database" (Illinois State Archives, 2001).

Many other libraries and archives have valuable collections. Some of these have useful Web sites. The Georgia Historical Society (www.georgiahistory.com/) site details the collections they archive and provides information regarding access. The North Carolina State Library (http://statelibrary.dcr.state.nc.us/iss/gr/NCSource.htm), for example, maintains an information Web page with links to North Carolina genealogical societies, North Carolina USGenWeb projects, and other useful sites. The researcher can use the library and archive finding tools discussed in Part 3 to locate the libraries or archives in the states that interest them.

Christine's Genealogy Web site (www.ccharity.com/) is described as the "Home base for African American Genealogical Research." Many census, cemetery, emancipation, and plantation records, as well as other transcriptions of slavery-related documents are either linked or searchable through this Web site. There are also great current research articles and an archive of past articles. Christine's own Charity family genealogical data and documentation are published on the site as well.

Christine's Genealogy Web site links to other African American research sites on the Web including the FreedMan's Bureau online at http://freedmansbureau.com. This site provides information and some searchable databases of data from the FreedMan's Bureau:

> "The Bureau of Refugees, Freedmen and Abandoned Lands, often referred to as the Freedmen's Bureau, was established in the War Department by an act of March 3, 1865. The Bureau supervised all relief and educational activities relating to refugees and freedmen, including issuing rations, clothing and medicine. The Bureau also assumed custody of confiscated lands or property in the former Confederate States, border states, District of Columbia, and Indian Territory. The bureau records were created or maintained by bureau headquarters, the assistant commissioners and the state superintendents of education and included personnel records and a variety of standard reports concerning bureau programs and conditions in the states" (FreedMan's Bureau, 2000).

Figure 4.8 is an index transcription from the Freedman's Bureau Online site "Register of Marriages in Tennessee" collection.

NARA holds some document collections that are invaluable for African American genealogy research. The NARA Web site (www.nara.gov/genealogy) lists the microfilmed records available and describes their general contents. The NARA records include:

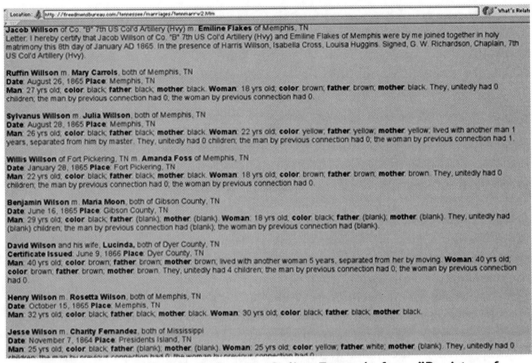

Figure 4.8. Freedman's Bureau Online Example from "Register of Marriages in Tennessee"

1. Freedman's Savings and Trust Company Records
2. Marriage Registers of Freedmen

Afrigeneas: African Ancestored Genealogy (www.afrigeneas.com/) is another metasite for researching African American genealogy using the Internet. The Afrigeneas site hosts census and primary document transcription projects and many chats and Web boards for discussion of African American genealogical research.

Our BlackHeritage.com (www.ourblackheritage.com/) provides searchable indexes and databases of historical documents, military records, censuses, and other sources useful for researching African American ancestors.

Native American Genealogical Research

All genealogical research has to start with an individual and work back through the generations. If an ancestor is discovered who is described in vital records as "Indian" or by a specific tribal affiliation, then you may need to begin research into resources specific to Native American/American Indian genealogy. Researchers looking for Native American ancestors must be knowledgeable of the historical relationships between the United States, Canada, Mexico, or South American countries, and the particular Native American group to which their ancestor belonged. They must also be aware of the legal relationships and key dates in the history of the legal relationships between the central, state, provincial, military, or local government—especially in the United States and Canada—and Native American groups and individuals.

"Indian ethnicity is a multi-faceted, complex issue. According to the 1990 U.S. Census, almost 2 million Americans describe themselves as Indian. Each tribe has its own regulations that determine who was considered a member of the tribe. These guidelines are occasionally modified and updated depending upon a tribe's special needs" (Kavasch, 1996:78).

Researchers may think they might have Native American/American Indian blood lines—that they are a "little bit Indian." This may or may not be the case. The researcher will need to research from the present until they encounter and document a Native American ancestor. They will also need to identify the tribal group with whom their ancestor was affiliated.

For example, in my family there has been a "story" that my maternal grandmother was part Cherokee because she was dark haired and small boned—in contrast to most of the rest of the family. The legend was that great-great Grandpa Wilson had met and married a Cherokee princess when he was trading horses in Tennessee. Reality, however, is rarely so picturesque, and documentation shows that great-great Grandpa Theodore Wilson married Caroline Lovell, a woman born of English parents in New York. Great-great Grandpa Theodore's parents were from Pennsylvania (per 1880 U.S. Census image viewed on Ancestry.com). My maternal grandmother's other grandparents, John and Rosina Schumm (Whorle), were both immigrants to the United States from Germany. So there is no Cherokee princess in that line after all.

A first question to ask is: "which Native American/American Indian tribe is being researched?" To say "Native American or American Indian genealogical research" is equivalent to saying "European genealogical research." This is not particularly helpful. You need to know which tribe your ancestor descended from, which geographical area they lived in, which language group they belonged to, and so on and work from there, much as is needed in working with international genealogical research.

"The term *tribe* describes a body of people bound together by blood relationships, perhaps speaking a common language or dialect, and occupying a definite territory. A tribe may also be socially, politically, and religiously affiliated with a village, a series of communities, or a widely scattered group of people who share a common heritage but not necessarily a tribal government. Many tribes also see themselves as nations, as they have been legally treated as tribal nations in the relationships and treaties with the U.S. government . . . More than 300 federally recognized Native American tribes in the United States are located on approximately 300 federal Indian reservations. Many additional tribes and groups, almost 200, most of them east of the Mississippi

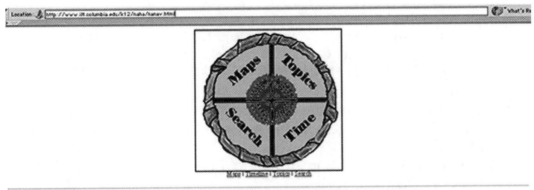

Figure 4.9. Native American Navigator Web Site

River, do not have federal recognition; yet a number of them have confederated, sharing common heritage and large western reservations" (Kavasch, 1996:53–54).

This definition can be expanded to take into account the native peoples of Canada, Mexico, and South America.

Once the researcher has identified and documented a Native American ancestor there are several good Internet resources that may help in continuing their research.

The Native American Navigator project (www.ilt.columbia.edu/k12/naha/nanav.html) on the ITL Web site (Institute for Learning Technologies at Columbia University) is a good place to start learning the historical background needed for productive Native American genealogy research (Figure 4.9).

The Heard Museum (www.heard.org/education/resource/htl.html) also provides a variety of information sources, including a Native American History timeline.

The original records of the headquarters of the Bureau of Indian Affairs are in the National Archives in Washington D.C., along with many records relating to Native Americans who maintained their tribal affiliations. The NARA Web site (www.nara.gov/genealogy) lists the microfilmed records available and describes their general contents. Most of the records, arranged by tribe, cover the years 1830 to 1940. The NARA records include:

- Indian Bounty Land Applications.
- Dawes Commission: 64,177 applications for enrollment in the Five Civilized Tribes (Cherokee, Chickasaw, Creek, and Seminole) submitted between 1898 and 1914. Note: there is no description in NAIL relating to the fifth tribe, Choctaw.
- Dawes Commission and the Enrollment of the Creeks.
- Final Rolls of the Citizens and Freedmen of the Five Civilized Tribes in Indian Territory.
- Index to the Final Rolls of Citizens and Freedmen of the Five Civilized Tribes in Indian Territory.
- Index to Applications Submitted for the Eastern Cherokee Roll of 1909 (Guion-Miller Roll).
- Wallace Roll of Cherokee Freedmen in Indian Territory, 1890.
- Kern-Clifton Roll of Cherokee Freedmen, January 16, 1867.
- 1896 Citizenship Applications: 9,618 applications received by the Dawes Commission.

Some of the NARA microfilm collections that support genealogical research for Native American ancestors have been partially digitized and are searchable through the NARA Archival Information Locator (NAIL) that was discussed in Parts 2 and 3. On the NARA Genealogy Web page under "Native American Records" the links for each collection connect to an appropriate area of the "Search Hints for Genealogical Data in NAIL" page and describe how to attempt locating the digitized images in the NARA system. For example, the "Final Rolls of the Citizens and Freedmen of the Five Civilized Tribes in Indian Territory" is searched by using the keyword "Final Rolls" and clicking on the box to check "Only Descriptions Linked to Digital Copies." Figures 4.10-4.12 are images of the progress from the simple index to the full displays of the results.

The Native American Documents Project (www.csusm.edu/nadp/nadp.htm) has begun indexing many of these documents. Ancestry.com has also indexed many of the NARA records collections. Anyone may search the indexes, but the entries are accessible to subscribers only.

The NativeWeb site (www.nativeweb.org/) is a central location for "Resources for Indigenous Cultures around the World." Their Genealogy (Tracing Roots) collection contains most of the major Native American genealogy Web sites including links to Arapahoe, Cherokee, Cheyenne, Colorado, and other specific tribal genealogy sites. Of special interest in this collection are links to major libraries and archives for Native American genealogy research. Most researchers will find that they will get their best documentation visiting libraries and archives that hold documents related to Native American genealogy research. Many researchers reach a successful conclusion to their research by corresponding with tribal organizations to request access to their records.

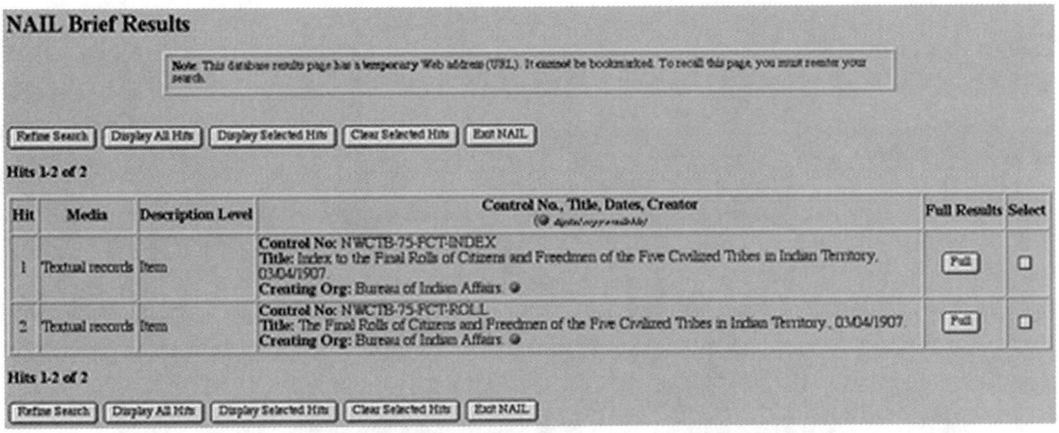

Figure 4.10. NAIL Brief Results Display Digitized Images from "
Final Rolls of the Citizens and Freedmen of the Five Civilized Tribes in
Indian Territory"

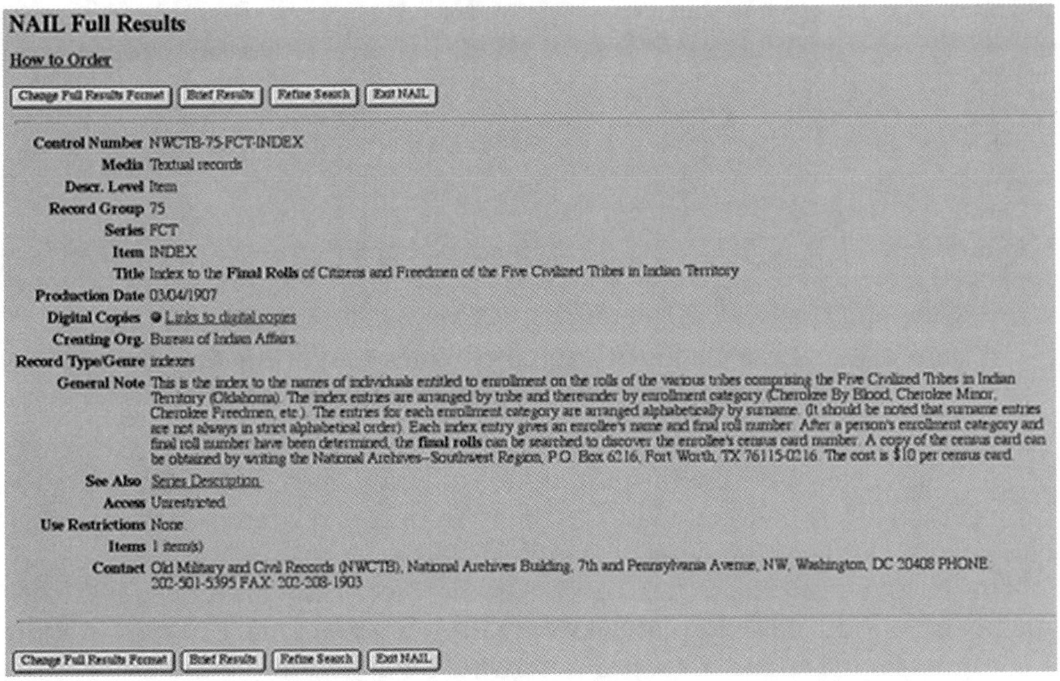

Figure 4.11. NAIL Results Display for "Final Rolls of the Citizens and
Freedmen of the Five Civilized Tribes in Indian Territory"

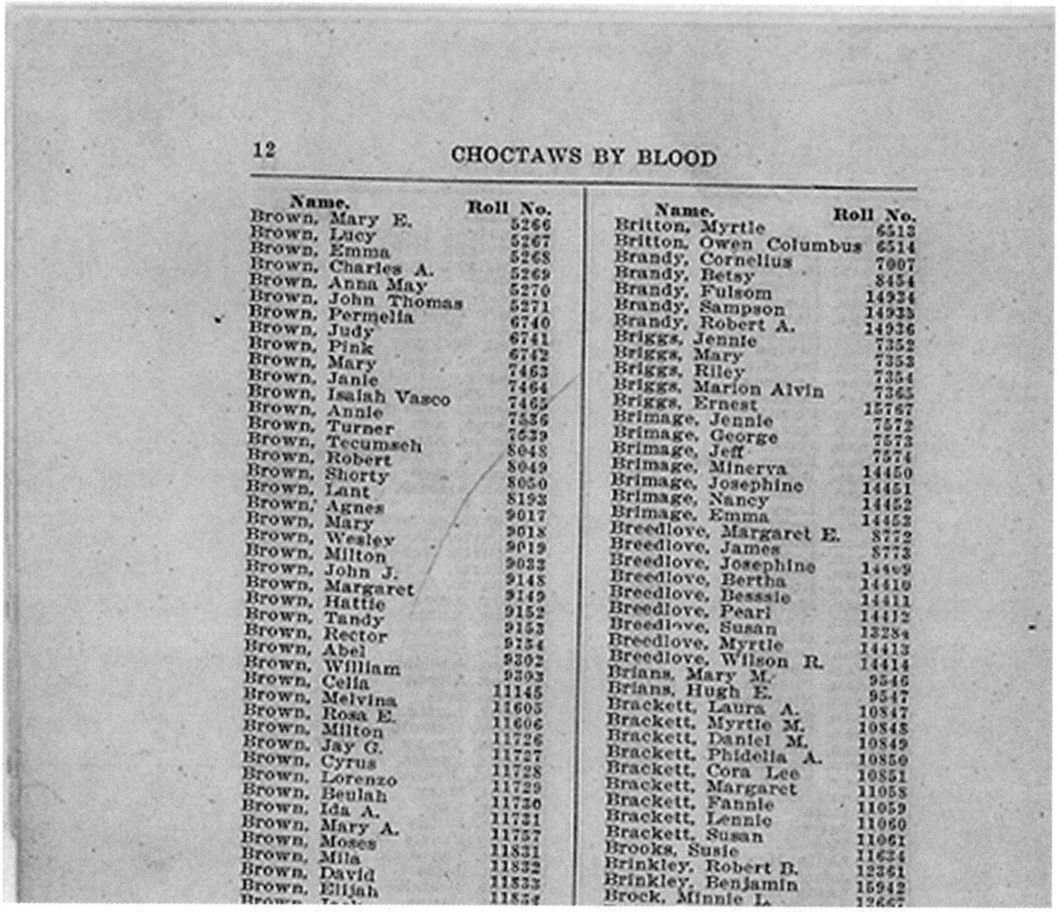

12 CHOCTAWS BY BLOOD

Name.	Roll No.
Brown, Mary E.	5266
Brown, Lucy	5267
Brown, Emma	5268
Brown, Charles A.	5269
Brown, Anna May	5270
Brown, John Thomas	5271
Brown, Permelia	6740
Brown, Judy	6741
Brown, Pink	6742
Brown, Mary	7463
Brown, Janie	7464
Brown, Isaiah Vasco	7465
Brown, Annie	7536
Brown, Turner	7639
Brown, Tecumseh	8048
Brown, Robert	8049
Brown, Shorty	8050
Brown, Lant	8193
Brown, Agnes	9017
Brown, Mary	9018
Brown, Wesley	9019
Brown, Milton	9033
Brown, John J.	9148
Brown, Margaret	9149
Brown, Hattie	9152
Brown, Tandy	9153
Brown, Rector	9154
Brown, Abel	9302
Brown, William	9303
Brown, Celia	11145
Brown, Melvina	11605
Brown, Rosa E.	11606
Brown, Milton	11726
Brown, Jay G.	11727
Brown, Cyrus	11728
Brown, Lorenzo	11729
Brown, Beulah	11730
Brown, Ida A.	11731
Brown, Mary A.	11757
Brown, Moses	11831
Brown, Mila	11832
Brown, David	11833
Brown, Elijah	11834

Name.	Roll No.
Britton, Myrtle	6513
Britton, Owen Columbus	6514
Brandy, Cornelius	7007
Brandy, Betsy	8454
Brandy, Fulsom	14934
Brandy, Sampson	14935
Brandy, Robert A.	14936
Briggs, Jennie	7352
Briggs, Mary	7353
Briggs, Riley	7354
Briggs, Marion Alvin	7365
Briggs, Ernest	15767
Brimage, Jennie	7572
Brimage, George	7573
Brimage, Jeff	7574
Brimage, Minerva	14450
Brimage, Josephine	14451
Brimage, Nancy	14452
Brimage, Emma	14453
Breedlove, Margaret E.	8772
Breedlove, James	8773
Breedlove, Josephine	14409
Breedlove, Bertha	14410
Breedlove, Bessie	14411
Breedlove, Pearl	14412
Breedlove, Susan	13284
Breedlove, Myrtle	14413
Breedlove, Wilson R.	14414
Brians, Mary M.	9546
Brians, Hugh E.	9547
Brackett, Laura A.	10847
Brackett, Myrtle M.	10848
Brackett, Daniel M.	10849
Brackett, Phidelia A.	10850
Brackett, Cora Lee	10851
Brackett, Margaret	11058
Brackett, Fannie	11059
Brackett, Lennie	11060
Brackett, Susan	11061
Brooks, Susie	11634
Brinkley, Robert B.	12361
Brinkley, Benjamin	15942
Brock, Minnie L.	[illegible]

Figure 4.12. Example Image from the "Final Rolls of the Citizens and Freemen of the Five Civilized Tribes in Indian Territory"

The NativeNet Web site (http://cs.fdl.cc.mn.us/natnet/) is a great source of information. They collect and link to many resources related to Native American history, culture, and current events.

The Native American Indian Genealogy Webring Homepage (http://members.tripod.com/~kjunkutie/natvrng.htm) is a great place to start looking for pages specific to the tribal group in which you are interested.

Heraldry

Heraldry or the recording and use of "coats of arms" is a popular topic for some genealogical researchers. It is also one area where there are many misunderstandings and frequent misrepresentations on the Internet. Certain companies and individuals try to sell products printed with "coats of arms" or "family crests" (the upper part of the design on a coat of arms) to anyone with a given surname and give them the impression that this is legitimate. They prey on genuine family pride to make their sales. The Genealogy Web site Watch Dog Committee" (www.ancestordetective.com/watchdog.htm) tracks these deceptive companies when they appear on the Internet. While they may not be perpetrating outright scams or frauds they are definitely misleading the people that spend their good money for these questionable products.

In formal legal and historical terms, there is no such thing as a "family" coat of arms. The right to bear a particular coat of arms is generally accorded to the direct descendants of a particular individual who was historically granted the rights to use a particular heraldic image or design. That individual descendant is described as "armigerous" or qualified by their documented genealogy to bear the coat of arms registered for descendants of their particular family with an official or accepted office of arms or armorial authorities. The complete history of heraldry is beyond the scope of this book, but several of the sites described below provide good background and in-depth discussion of this topic.

"To the extent that heraldry affects genealogy, it is in the context of tracing armigerous ancestors. Arms, once granted by appropriate authority, are inherited from the person granted the right to use them. Since this right must be registered, a wide variety of heraldic sources exists to trace armigerous lineages back to the original grantee—even, with proper documentation, into the Middle Ages. Unfortunately for genealogy, the right to use coats of arms (sometimes incorrectly called "crests") is widely misunderstood. Many people who become interested in their ancestors turn first to published armorial dictionaries, typically those by Burke or Debrett, to discover whether someone who shares their surname once used a coat of arms. Those untutored in heraldry and genealogy sometimes guess that they are descended from that person. Others assume they have the right to use arms once granted to anyone with their surname" (Hinchliff, 1999: 6).

Only certain individuals are entitled to display a coat of arms and most of those are residents of the United Kingdom and Europe. However, that doesn't mean that we can't have our own coats of arms created and registered.

The American College of Heraldry (http://members.aol.com/ballywoodn/acheraldry.html) is a non-profit chartered organization that has been operating since 1972. It is recommended by the Genealogical Web Site Watchdog Committee (http://ancestordetective.com/watchdog.htm#Coats). This site offers "an introduction to the study and perpetuation of Heraldry in the United States and abroad." It also offers some excellent tutorials and explanations of heraldic traditions and definitions of terms (Figure 4.13). But, the most valuable thing about this site is that it offers assistance in designing a unique coat of arms for the researcher. The American College of Heraldry then announces the coat of arms and maintains a directory of these coats of arms and the individuals who are entitled to bear them. The American College of Heraldry will also work with individuals to register a coat of arms recognized by "major offices of arms abroad" or unrecognized coats of arms appropriately. The

Figure 4.13. American College of Heraldry

most famous of these "major offices of arms abroad" is the College of Arms (www.college-of-arms.gov.uk), the official office of arms for the United Kingdom:

> "The College of Arms is the official repository of coats of arms and pedigrees of English, Welsh, Northern Irish and Commonwealth families and their descendants. Its records also include official copies of the records of Ulster King of Arms the originals of which remain in Dublin . . . The officers of the College, known as heralds, specialize in genealogical and heraldic work for their respective clients" (College of Arms, 2001).

This is the organization to work with when the researcher believes that a

DOROTHY L

AS OUR WHIMSY TAKES US

dorothyl@kentvm.kent.edu

Figure 4.14. Picture of the DOROTHYL Crest

connection to an Irish, British, Welsh, or Scottish ancestor entitles them to bear a coat of arms. The College of Arms will also assist researchers to research coats of arms from other European nations.

The D'Addezio Genealogy Web site (www.daddezio.com/genealogy/articles/registry.html) has published an article by Linda Mock that discusses and lists coats of arms registries in a number of nations.

Designing one's own "coat of arms" can be a fun and educational activity. Many good teachers ask students to design their own coat of arms using their imagination and knowledge of their family, as part of historical or genealogical research projects. Some few teachers make the mistake of having students look for a coat of arms for their surnames. An example of a fun "coat of arms" is found for the Internet mailing list DOROTHYL that has its own "coat of arms." DOROTHYL (http://listserv.kent.edu/dorothyl) is a discussion of mystery literature. In 1993/94 Hilde Horvath of Cook College, Rutgers the State University, Deb Whitney, aka "Auntie Lil"—one of the original members of the group, and several other list members designed the "coat of arms" reproduced in Figure 4.14. The design honors Dorothy L. Sayers as it is based on the fictional "coat of arms" described in her stories as belonging to the family of her character Lord Peter Wimsey. Hilde Horvath started a tradition of ordering DOROTHYL t-shirts with the DOROTHYL coat-of-arms silk screened on them and made available to list members at cost. Each year coffee mugs with the DOROTHYL "coat-of-arms" are designed and produced for subscribers to order at cost as well. Nancy Whitney, daughter of Deb Whitney, continues the tradition after the untimely passing of her mother in 1998.

Lineage Societies

Some genealogical researchers are looking to document an ancestral connection that will gain them membership in a particular lineage society. Each lineage society has their own particular rules governing membership and the documentation required for application for membership. Many of these lineage societies have Web sites on which they publish their membership requirements and application instructions. Cyndi's List (www.cyndislist.com) has compiled the most comprehensive directory of lineage society Web sites. Cyndi's Lineage Societies category listings range from the "Associated Daughters of Early American Witches" (www.adeaw.org/) to "The United Empire Loyalists' Association of Canada" (www.npiec.on.ca/~uela/uela1.htm) and everything in between.

One of the most famous of lineage societies is the National Society Daughters of the American Revolution (DAR) (www.dar.org/). Their Web site (Figure 4.15) is exemplary in providing complete detail about membership requirements, the history, purpose, and current activities of the organization:

"Any woman is eligible for membership who is no less than eighteen years of age and can prove lineal, blood line descent from an ancestor who aided in achieving American independence. She must provide documentation for each statement of birth, marriage, and death" (www.dar.org/natsociety/membership.html).

The national DAR Web site also links to the Web sites of individual chapters or provides basic contact information for chapters without Web sites. The DAR's genealogy and history library catalog is also online and searchable. The DAR library, as discussed in Part 3, is one of the most valuable resources for genealogy researchers.

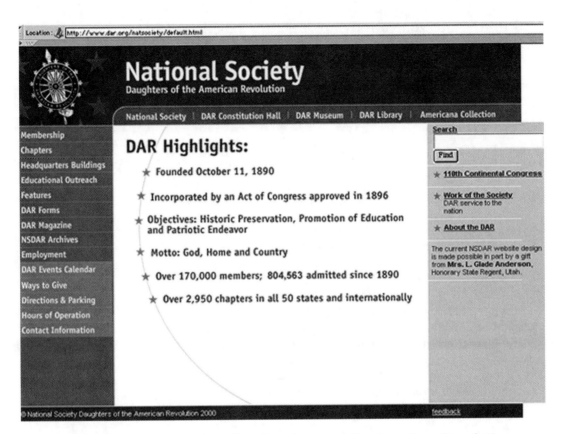

Figure 4.15. National Society Daughters of the American Revolution

Genealogical researchers in the United States and Canada will frequently need to continue their research internationally. Knowledge of both world and regional history, as well as some basic language skills are required to do this. Researchers identifying and documenting African American ancestors must be aware of the history and legal ramifications of slavery, the legal end of slavery, and the subsequent legal treatment of African Americans in terms of their rights and recognition as U.S. citizens in census and other vital records. Researchers identifying and documenting Native American ancestors must also be aware of the history and legal relationship between their national, state, provincial, and local governments and the Native American groups with which their ancestors were affiliated. There are many good supporting resources on the Internet that will aid researchers in these three areas.

Many wonderful resources for genealogical research are appearing on the Internet even as this is being written. The Web-based workshop companion to this book will give you and your patrons an opportunity to use the resources described in this text to do their own personal research. Because the workshop is on the Web, it can and will be updated as new resources appear. As you and your patrons work with these resources, you will discover new Web sites that serve special research purposes. The Web-based workshop includes a form to share your positive or negative experiences in working with the resources in the workshop or those discovered by you and your patrons. With your permission, your experiences will be shared with other readers and workshop participants in the true spirit of Internet research.

References

Brown, R.M. 1994. *Murder at Monticello*. New York: Bantam Books.

College of Arms. 2001. [Online]. Available: www.college-of-arms.gov.uk [2001, October 23].

FreedMan's Bureau. 2000. [Online]. Available: http://freedmansbureau.com/ [2001, October 23].

Harrington, J. 1995. *The Death of Cousin Rose*. Aurora, Colo.: Write Way Publishing.

Hinchliff, H. 1999. "A Right to Bear Arms? An Examination of Commercial Offerings for Henderson of St. Laurence, Scotland." *National Genealogical Society Quarterly* 87 (March): 6-9.

Illinois State Archives. 2001. [Online]. Available: www.cyberdriveillinois.com/departments/archives/servant.html [2001, October 23].

Immigration and Naturalization Service. 2001. [Online]. Available: www.ins.usdoj.gov/graphics/aboutins/history/index.htm [2001, October 23].

Kavasch, E.B. 1996. *A Student's Guide to Native American Genealogy*. Phoenix, Ariz.: Oryx Press.

Pratchett, T. 1996. *Feet of Clay*. New York: Harper Collins.

Success Story 4.1   Networking and Data-Sharing with Living Relatives in Europe and the U.S.

Larry Naukam lnaukam@libraryweb.org (Outreach and Extension/Genealogy and Local History Librarian, Rochester, New York Public Library, Internet Genealogy Researcher - Volunteer German Translator)

The Internet is not yet a major source of easily accessible and organized data (like one could find in a library collection), but it was invaluable in providing a communication mechanism for me to share data with my living relatives through e-mail and a shared Web site. The Internet simplified communications and data sharing with living relatives in Europe, as well as the United States.

Every time I think about the connections that have been made, it gives a warm feeling that merely filling in a pedigree chart never could. It's changed all our lives in a small but pleasant way, connecting us in this unconnected world. The Internet allowed us to meet, collaborate, share data, and organize our family reunions. It WOULD NOT HAVE HAPPENED without the net. Our lives are richer for it.

My mother's maiden name was Krautwurst. I had gotten an e-mail from Fred K, a minister living at that time in Montgomery, Ala. He was on Compuserve (back when it mattered and was a player) and had corresponded with Terry K, who lived in North Carolina and is an organic farming/children's book author. I had actually met Terry's brother Lon, in Rochester, N.Y.

Terry wrote to Fred that he didn't know much about the K family except his own; but his brother Lon knew me, and maybe I could help Fred. Fred wrote to me via e-mail. I said, sure, pardner, I have 15 generations on the family. Where do you guys fit in?

Fred's family settled in Washington, DC. (You can see where the "free" e-mail of the net makes all of this possible quickly and cheaply). He sent me the e-mail of his sister, Linda K—who is born on my exact birthday. She's an elementary school teacher. She then sent me a large amount of family data—and I might add, made up a questionnaire about the family that she sent to and got responses from all of her family. This is much more than I ever would have gotten cold. Her family data pointed out that while their family is from Neu Werbass, Serbia (now), their progenitor was from Schaafheim, Hessen, Germany. (This appeared in several history books published about Neu Werbass.)

I had visited Schaafheim and had already met the "live cousins" there. I had copies of articles that appeared in the local newspapers there at the time of my visit, which essentially had noted that "descendant of local family returns to ancestral home." I found Linda's Werbass progenitor already in my database as "emigrated to Serbia" in the old German records. I gave her another 11 generations back to the earliest ancestors that I have found.

Subsequently, I traveled to their family reunion in Washington, and had a nice reception showing them my pictures and collection of Schaafheimiana.

I wrote this up and sent the data and info to my German cousin, Otto K—a retired steel engineer who happens to be the local historian and president of the Heimageschichteverein (local history group) in Schaafheim. He pointed out that they have people from Serbia who were tossed out of there after WW II—the "fluchtlinge"—and he knows about a Werbasser old town group.

He sent me the address of Liesel Krautwurst in the U.S.A. She was a woman born in Werbass in the twenties. He also sent me a wall chart from 1935, done when Liesel was 15, which someone had in their possession in Schaafheim for the last 60 plus years. I wrote to Liesel. "I got your address from Otto—would you like to correspond?" She replied with a tentative "yes" back. I wrote, "I am sending something under paper mail which I believe belongs to you." I sent the chart.

A week later, a sea chest-sized package, I kid you not, of cookies, cakes, etc. arrived at my house. "Thank you so much for that chart. I thought that I had lost it back in 1935." Her family had never known about it—not her children, nor grandchildren and great-grandchildren. Now they do. Later, I visited her and her family. Her grandson Ron then came with me to a reunion in Schaafheim, where Margaret tells the story mentioned next.

Margaret Krautwurst was in a concentration camp after the war (where the German settlers had been placed) and cared for the newborn daughter of Liesel Krautwurst; that daughter grew up to be Ron Wagner's mother. I was in the middle at the reunion, listening to Margaret tell me in German, with me telling Ron in English, the story his mother and grandmother never told him. I will remember that night for my whole life.

After returning home I put the personal pages up and as a result (having told the Germans at the reunion there, 30 of whom had net access) I get contacted by Lori Schiffler and David Croutworst (note the variant spelling).

Lori is a born Werbasser who was expelled from Serbia. I wrote an article for her for the Werbasser Zeitung. When I visited Liesel (the old lady referred to above) I used the Web (FEEFHS.org) to get background info on Werbass and learned about the atrocities committed there and the gruesome way some of her family were killed.

David C. found my site on the Web, e-mailed me, and as a result I visit him. His family originally spelled their name Krautwurst. They have old German documents that no one there can read. I visited them, and translated the old docs for them, and they learned where their family comes from! His father is elderly and in poor health, and this made him very happy indeed.

So now, the Web has provided disparate parts of this family to come together. Gary Osthoff from South Africa e-mailed me, as did Reinhard Volker from Germany, Bernhard Braun from Pirmasens, and Fred Krautwurst (another one) from Vienna and the Netherlands! Search engines provide a source for these people to find the Web pages, and there is an e-mail link set up. There are also several pages that I translated into German for non-English speakers.

Still with me? I set up a site at myfamily.com to handle more pictures. Henry K. from Washington sets up his site to make it easy to plan out reunions. The URL for Henry Krautwurst is at: www.homestead.com/krautwurst/reunion2000.html.

In sum then, we have had all these people meet, join, share information and pictures, and use my open site and the myfamily passworded site, and now Henry's site to get together. Henry set up a signup sheet on the Web, where we all signed up for the reunion in 2000.

As a follow-up, the Croutworst clan referred to above brought their patriarch to the reunion. They were warmly welcomed as family, and the whole group had a wonderful time. Later on I got a card from them explaining that it had almost been a spiritual homecoming (Albert Croutworst is a retired minister), as well as a party. The family had been rejoined with far-flung relatives and warmly welcomed. The Fred Krautwurst (number two) above from Holland came to the 1998 reunion. He and his wife were childless by choice. I think that the "connection" made there might have influenced their decision to have two beautiful little kids since then. Maybe not, but he was a man with little interest in connections to the past, and they too were welcomed as family to our group. Now he has a family of his own.

The ability to meet other family members interested in genealogy and research, share data and photographs, research the history, (I must point out that none of the actual family data was on the Web. It has all been extracted from American and German hard copy resources) and plan reunions has been very much made possible by the use of the Internet. Time and distance have melted away and allowed us to share as if we were close in location, as well as by family ties.

Success Story 4.2   How African American and Native American Genealogy Researchers Begin with Internet Research Tools

Deborah Keener deb.keener@wayne.lib.oh.us (Head of Genealogy and Local History, Wayne County Public Library)

Genealogy researchers searching for African American or Native American ancestors using the Internet have basically the same resources available to them as any other genealogy researcher.

A few months ago, a researcher visited our Genealogy and Local History Department of the Wayne County Public Library in Wooster, Ohio looking for his African American ancestors from Alabama and Mississippi. He had some names and approximate dates. Using the Social Security Death Index, we were able to find the name of his grandfather, his place of death, and the month and year he died. Knowing this information, I encouraged him to contact the Health Department in Barberton, Ohio to obtain a copy of his death certificate. His grandfather's death certificate would give the specific death date. I was able to obtain the address and phone number for the Health Department through the Internet. Once the exact date of death would be determined, the researcher could contact the public library to find an obituary on his grandfather. The contact information for the public library could be obtained through the Internet, too. Many times, these obituaries include very useful information, such as parents' names, the place of birth of the deceased, and any survivors.

The researcher's grandfather was born in Alabama and his grandmother was born in Mississippi. Here in our local library, these two states are outside the scope of our collection. Once again, the Internet helped out. Through the Vital Records Web site, we were able to obtain the contact information for the health departments in the two corresponding states. By obtaining the birth records of his grandparents, he would be able to go back an additional generation.

Genealogy researchers searching for Native American ancestors can use tools such as the SSDI, the NARA full-text databases such as the Dawes Commission Records, the Land Bounty Applications, and the Index and Final Rolls of the Citizens and Freedmen of the Five Civilized Tribes in Indian Territory. But they can also find Web sites that list records and print resources and postal addresses, or e-mail addresses to write to for further information about data held in archives, libraries, or records maintained by tribal organizations. They can also find information to use in planning visits to the physical locations of archives, libraries, or records maintained by tribal groups.

Activity 4.1. Locating Internet Resources for International Genealogical Research

Overview:

In this activity you will review three metasites that select and list International Genealogical information Web sites. Choose a country, region, or ethnic group that you wish to focus on, or use Hungary.

STEP 1. Use your Web browser to connect to Cyndi's List http://www.cyndislist.com.

STEP 2. Click on "Main Index" and scroll down to browse for the country, region, or ethnic group of your choice. OR use the Search option to search for your choice.

STEP 3. What country, region, or ethnic group did you choose? Did Cyndi's List contain an index category that either explicitly named your chosen place or group or a broader category that included it?

STEP 4. Click on the index category or categories that suit your chosen place or group. How many and what kinds of sites are listed? Do they seem as though they will be useful for genealogical research?

STEP 5. Click on one of the sites under the Cyndi's List category you've chosen. What site did you connect to? What do you think of the value of the site you chose for genealogical research focused on the place or group you chose?

STEP 6. Use your Web browser to connect to WorldGenWeb Web site. http://worldgenweb.org.

STEP 7. Use the country or region you used in Steps 1-5. If you used an ethnic group use the most central location for that ethnic group. Click on the region or the region that contains your country (e.g., Eastern Europe to search for Hungary) and use the "A-Z" index to select your country directly.

STEP 8. How many and what kinds of links are listed under your country or region? (e.g., "Eastern Europe" has a link for most Eastern European countries, mailing lists, and a map tool link)
Will the information you found on the WorldGenWeb pages for your location be useful for genealogical research?

STEP 9. Use your Web browser to connect to Everton's Genealogical Helper: International Genealogy Resources page http://everton.com/reference/world-resource.php.

STEP 10. Read through the countries listed on this page. Is the country or

	a country in the region you chose in Step 6 listed? If it is click on it in the index. If your country is not listed click on "Hungary."
STEP 11.	How many and what kinds of sites are listed under your country? Do they seem as though they will be useful for genealogical research?
STEP 12.	Which of these three metasites will you be most likely to use to locate high quality international genealogy research Web sites?

Note: If you are working self-paced and would like instructor feedback e-mail your responses and questions to *diane@kovacs.com*

Activity 4.2. Researching African American Genealogy on the Internet

Overview:

In this activity you will review three metasites that review and list Internet sources of African American Genealogical information, including sources of historical and legal information.

STEP 1. Use your Web browser to connect to Christine's Genealogy Web site http://www.ccharity.com/.

STEP 2. Read through the main page. Then click on the link "Contents." Read through the contents.

STEP 3. Click on a link that interests you, for example "Manumission papers," and read through the materials available. Click through to a document. What did you look at? Who provided this transcription?

STEP 4. Go back to the Christine's Genealogy Web site main page and click on the link "Links." Read through the categories available, then click on a category of your choice. What category did you click on? What kinds of sites are listed?

STEP 5. Go back to the Christine's Genealogy Web site main page and look for the link to "Searchable Databases." Read through the listing then click on the link for "The Freedman's Bureau Online." The direct URL is http://freedmensbureau.com/.

STEP 6. Read through this page. What kinds of resources are available? Click on a resource of your choice. What resource did you click on? What kind of information did you find?

STEP 7. Use your Web browser to connect to Afrigeneas: African Ancestored Genealogy http://www.afrigeneas.com/.

STEP 8. Read through this page. Note the searching and browsing options. Note also that Afrigeneas is also an Internet discussion list.
Scroll all the way down the main page until you see the list of "Affiliated Sites" and you should also see the index of the Web site.

STEP 9. Look under the category "Library." Click on the link for "Georgia Slave Bills of Sale." Read through this material. What is this? Who is the author? What is the source of this information? Do you think this will be useful for researchers looking for information about African American ancestors?

STEP 10.   Go back to the Afrigeneas main page and browse through links of your choice.

STEP 11.   Use your Web browser to connect to Our BlackHeritage.com http://www.ourblackheritage.com/.

STEP 12.   Read carefully through the contents of this page. Look for and click on the link "Free Born" Slave Certification-December 22, 1841 (A document certifying that "Eliza Rector, age about fourteen years, is a free person." Dated Dec. 22, 1841)

How would a researcher use the information provided in this document?*

Note: this is a pdf file requiring the Adobe Acrobat reader.

*The family of Eliza Rector may find this information useful.

STEP 13.   Look for and click on the link "Slave Rental Agreement/Receipt-January 8, 1857 (Images of a rental agreement/receipt for the rental of a slave)"

How would a researcher use the information provided in this document?*

Note: this is a pdf file requiring the Adobe Acrobat reader.

*The slave owner's name is mentioned and that may be used to trace the family of Jim.

STEP 14.   Which of these three metasites will you be most likely to use to locate high quality African American genealogy research information?

Note: If you are working self-paced and would like instructor feedback e-mail your responses and questions to *diane@kovacs.com*

Activity 4.3. Using the NARA Web Site and Other Internet Resources for Native American Genealogical Research

Overview:

In this activity you will use the NARA Web site to locate and view scanned images of records that may be helpful for Native American genealogical research. You will also review three Native American Genealogical metasites.

STEP 1.   Use your Web browser to connect to The NARA Genealogy Page *http://www.nara.gov/genealogy*.

STEP 2.   Scroll down the page or use your browser's Find option to go to "Native American Records."
Read through the records available.

STEP 3.   Click on the link for "1896 Citizenship Applications: 9,618 applications received by the Dawes Commission."
Read through the "Search Hint" and then click on "Search NAIL" and follow the instructions for the sample search name: J. M. Abercrombye.
Click on "Display Results." Read through the record displayed. Click on "Full" to display the full document. What kind of information is included in this document? Is there a digitized copy of the document available?

STEP 4.   Repeat Step 3 choosing a Native American Records series that interests you or search the 1896 Citizenship applications using a different name.

STEP 5.   Use your Web browser to connect to The NativeWeb site *http://www.nativeweb.org/*.

STEP 6.   Read through this page carefully. Then either scroll down and look at the resource categories index or click on the link for "Resource Center." Read through the categories.

STEP 7.   Click on the link "Genealogy (Tracing Roots)." How many sites are listed? Choose two of these sites and click through to visit them. Which sites did you choose? Why? Did the sites provide information that you think will be useful to a researcher looking for information about a Native American ancestor?

STEP 8.   Use your Web browser to connect to The NativeNet Web site *http://cs.fdl.cc.mn.us/natnet/*.

STEP 9.   Read through this page. Then click on "Info Links." Are there any sites listed that might be useful for genealogy research on Native American ancestors? Click through on those links that you think might be useful. Which sites did you select?

Which sites would be useful in learning historical and legal background information? Click through on those links that you think might be useful. Which sites did you select?

STEP 10. Use your Web browser to connect to Native American Indian Genealogy Webring Homepage *http://members.tripod.com/ ~kjunkutie/natvrng.htm.*

STEP 11. Read through this page. This is the coordinating page for a Webring. Webrings are groups of voluntarily affiliated Web sites. Click on "Want to see who's in the Ring?"

STEP 12. How many sites are in this Webring? Choose two sites and click through and review each site. Which two sites did you choose? Do you think either of these sites will be helpful for Native American genealogy research? How or how not?

STEP 13. Click back to the main Native American Indian Genealogy Webring Homepage. Click on the link "Other Useful Links." Read through these links.

STEP 14. Which of these sites (NARA and the three metasites) will you be most likely to use to locate high quality Native American genealogy research information? Why?

Note: If you are working self-paced and would like instructor feedback e-mail your responses and questions to *diane@kovacs.com*

Activity 4.4. Learning about Heraldry and Lineage Societies on the Internet

Overview:

In this activity you will search for information and support for Heraldry and Lineage Societies.

Web-based readings:

1. "The Meaning of Arms"—http://members.aol.com/ballywoodn/acheraldry.html#meaning.
2. "Coat of Arms Registries" by Linda Mock on the D'Addezio Genealogy Web site—www.daddezio.com/genealogy/articles/registry.html.

STEP 1.	Use your Web browser to connect to Cyndi's List *http://www.cyndislist.com.*
STEP 2.	Click on "Main Index" and scroll down to browse for the "Heraldry" category OR use the Search option to search for your "Heraldry" and click on the result for the category "Heraldry."
STEP 3.	Browse through the list of sites that support Heraldry studies or interests. How many and what types of Web sites are listed?
STEP 4.	Click on a Heraldry link that interests you. Which link did you click on? Will this site be useful for your research?
STEP 5.	Use your Web browser to connect to The American College of Heraldry Web site *http://members.aol.com/ballywoodn/acheraldry.html.* What is the purpose of this organization? What services do they offer? Who are the people responsible for these services?
STEP 6.	Use your Web browser to connect to the College of Arms *http://www.college-of-arms.gov.uk.* What is the purpose of this organization? What services do they offer? Who are the people responsible for these services?
STEP 7.	What differences do you note between the types of service and the nature of these two organizations? (e.g., one is a government agency and the other is a non-profit organization)
STEP 8.	Click on "Main Index" again and scroll down to browse for the "Societies & Groups" category OR use the Search option to search for your "Lineage Societies."
STEP 9.	Browse through the list of lineage society sites. How many and what types of societies are listed?

153

STEP 10.   Click on a lineage society link that interest you. Which link did you click on? What interests you in this society? What is the purpose of this organization? What are the membership requirements? Who are the people responsible for this group?

STEP 11.   Use your Web browser to connect to the National Society Daughters of the American Revolution Web site *http://www.dar.org.*

STEP 12.   How does the DAR site compare—in quantity and types of information, research tool, membership requirements, purpose, and benefits of membership—to the site you linked to in Step 10?

Note: If you are working self-paced and would like instructor feedback e-mail your responses and questions to *diane@kovacs.com*

Sources

The Internet Genealogy Ready-Reference E-Library

(Links to sites mentioned in this book—this e-library is on the Internet at www.kovacs.com/ns/genlibrary.html)

The e-library will continue to grow and be updated. As these sites are discussed in-depth in the text, the sites listed here are annotated only if their title isn't explanatory.

Contents:

Part 1. Selected Basic Genealogical Research Tutorials

"20 Ways to Avoid Genealogical Grief"

http://www.rootsweb.com/roots-l/20ways.html
These great tips for genealogical research were originally authored by Margaret M. Sharon (margaret@sfu.ca).

"First Steps: Genealogy for Beginners"

http://www.lineages.com/FirstSteps/
Lineages, Inc. basic tutorial for beginning genealogy researchers. Includes family interview toolkit.

"Getting Started"

http://www.ngsgenealogy.org/getstart/body_frame.html
The National Genealogical Society's tutorial for genealogical reseach beginners. It begins with the question "Why Genealogy." Click on "Suggestions for Beginners," which advises setting out what you already know and asking your family what they know. This tutorial is free and online. NGS also offers a home study course and a more in-depth online workshop for fee.

"Guide to Tracing Family Trees"

http://rwguide.rootsweb.com/
One of the most comprehensive genealogy research tutorials. The guide starts with advice and guidance for beginners and then also offers information for more advanced genealogical researchers.

"How Do I Begin?"

http://www.familysearch.org/Eng/Search/RG/guide/all_t3_resmeth_-_how_do_i_begin.asp
This tutorial is very practical and clear. Each step is explained. The site is offered by the Church of Jesus Christ of Latter Day Saints, which has a long history of assisting genealogists.

"Immigration and Ships Passenger Lists Research Guide"

http://home.att.net/~arnielang/shipgide.html
"The goal of this Guide is to help in research of immigration records and ship's passenger lists, both on-line and off-line. The emphasis is on helping those who may be new to this research, but it includes tips, links, and help that may be of interest to all. This Guide is based on material originally prepared for the Genealogical Society of Bergen County, N.J." (accessed 2001, October 23).

"Learning about Genealogy and the Internet"

http://www.scls.lib.wi.us/mcm/programs/genealogyconnectat.html
Heart O' Wisconsin Genealogical Society Tutorial for using the Internet for Genealogy Research hosted by the McMillan Memorial Library in Wisconsin Rapids, Wisconsin.

Part 1. Sites for Evaluating Genealogical Information on the Internet

Ancestry.com Articles:

Morgan, G.G. 2001. "Bogus Genealogies." *Ancestry Daily News.* 1/19/2001. http://www.ancestry.com/library/view/news/articles/3224.asp

Neil, M.J. 2001. "It's on 1,000 Web Sites." *Ancestry Daily News.* 1/17/2001. http://www.ancestry.com/library/view/news/articles/3202.asp

Ancestor Detective Genealogical Web Site Watchdog

http://www.ancestordetective.com/watchdog.htm

Cyndi's List Category: Myths, Hoaxes, and Scams

http://www.CyndisList.com/myths.htm
(Note: Read through the information under the sub-categories: Common Genealogical Myths, as well as Other Myths, Hoaxes & Scams)

International Black Sheep Society of Genealogists Hall of Shame

http://blacksheep.rootsweb.com/shame.html
(Note: Page down until you see the list of "bad" Web sites or Web sites where problems have been reported.)

Genealogy Fraud/Fraudulent Lineages

http://www.linkline.com/personal/xymox/fraud/fraud.htm

National Genealogical Society's Genealogical Standards

http://www.ngsgenealogy.org/comstandards.htm
Required reading for any serious genealogical researcher or librarian.

Part 2. The Ten "Best" Genealogical Ready-Reference Tools

1. Social Security Death Records Index (SSDI)

http://www.rootsweb.org
http://www.ancestry.com
The SSDI is searchable on other sites, but these two have good currency and advanced search tools.

2. Vital Records Information for All States and Territories of the United States & International

http://www.vitalrec.com/
Comprehensive listing of Vital Records sources and access guidelines for site on the Internet or otherwise. Collected and maintained by Elizabeth Orsay (vitalrecords@usa.net).

3. FamilySearch - How to Do a Family History and List of Where to Find (LDS) Family History Centers

http://www.familysearch.org

This is the LDS church's (Mormon) searchable full-text collection of family history records and materials and links to helpful genealogical research.

4. American Family Immigration History Center

http://www.ellisislandrecords.org/

Ellis Island records online and searchable.

5. RootsWeb Genealogical Data Cooperative

http://www.rootsweb.com

The oldest and most comprehensive Web site for genealogy resources. Sponsors and links to Cyndi's List and many other outstanding projects. (See Also Immigrant Ships Transcriber's Guide, USGenWeb, WorldGenWeb, Genconnect)

6. USGenWeb Project

http://www.usgenweb.com/

All volunteer coordinated state by state/county by county projects to put full-text genealogy materials online. Including: cemetery records, census data, family histories, newspapers, diaries, and more.

7. Ancestry.com

http://www.ancestry.com

8. GENDEX—WWW Genealogical Index

http://www.gendex.com/gendex/

9. Cyndi's Genealogy Homepage

http://www.CyndisList.com/

Most comprehensive selective collection of genealogical Web sites known. Strongly recommended by genealogy researchers and librarians.

10. National Archives and Records Administration (NARA): The Genealogy Page

http://www.nara.gov/genealogy

Includes online catalogs of microfilm collections. Microfilm is available at the National Archives Building in Washington, D.C., at NARA's 13 regional records services facilities, and through our Microfilm Rental Program. Please note that many large libraries and genealogical societies have purchased all or some of the microfilm sets.

Part 2. Other Useful Genealogical Reference Sites

AccessGenealogy
http://www.accessgenealogy.com/
Some scanned images of genealogical books and documents available free on the Web as the "Free Online Genealogy Library."

Altavista and Google Web Search Engines
http://www.altavista.com
http://www.google.com
These two perform very well in retrieving genealogy specific Web sites. Google shines in this area of searching.

Family Tree Maker Online
http://www.familytreemaker.com/index.html
Commercial site with online indexes to their CD-ROM stored genealogical data. Good articles for beginners and advanced genealogical researchers.

Finding Treasures in the U.S. Census—Judy Hanna
http://www.firstct.com/fv/uscensus.html
Article about the genealogical and other research data to be found in the U.S. Census data files.

Genealogy.Org
http://www.genealogy.org/
Metasite that keeps track of the most popular/most frequently visited genealogical Web sites.

Helm's Genealogy Toolbox
http://genealogy.tbox.com/genealogy.html

Internet Public Library
http://www.ipl.org
Internet reference collection maintained by library volunteers and library school students.

Lee County Illinois USGenweb
http://www.rootsweb.com/~illee/index.htm
The Lee County Illinois volunteers have transcribed many useful files and created surname indexes for Lee County histories and newspapers.

Librarian's Index to the Internet
http://www.lii.org
Internet reference collection maintained by library volunteers.

Obituary Central
http://www.obitcentral.com/
Metasite focused on obituary sites.

OPLIN's Genealogy Gleanings and Collection
by Donovan Ackley
http://www.oplin.lib.oh.us
Donovan is a former genealogy librarian and an experienced genealogy researcher. This collection is well-chosen and annotated. The Genealogy Gleanings columns contain useful tips and advice for genealogical researchers.

Radix Hungarian Genealogy site
http://www.bogardi.com/gen/

SurnameWeb
http://www.surnameweb.com
Genealogy resource metasite searchable by surnames.

UMI "Genealogy & Local History Online"
http://genealogy.umi.com/
Library subscription-only database of scanned newspaper, book, and other document collections related to genealogy and local history.

United States Historical Census Data Browser
http://icg.fas.harvard.edu/~census/
Census by census details about the statistical and specific information gathered in each census.

The U.S. Census Bureau Gazetteer
http://www.census.gov/cgi-bin/gazetteer

VitalCheck
http://www.vitalcheck.com
Commercial site that provides online or telephone ordering of selected vital records for some states.

Part 3. Genealogy Communications Tools (Including references from Putting Your Family History Information on the Web section)

(See also National Genealogical Society's Genealogical Standards http://www.ngsgenealogy.org/comstandards.htm)
(See also RootsWeb http://www.rootsweb.org)

(See also USGenWeb http://www.usgenweb.org)
(See also WorldGenWeb http://worldgenweb.org)
(See also Ancestry.com http://www.ancestry.com groups and family trees)

AllFam: Some American Families and Their Origins
http://homepages.rootsweb.com/~allfam/

AnyWho
http://www.anywho.com
Search tool for e-mail, postal addresses, and telephone numbers.

Association of Professional Genealogists
http://www.apgen.org
Web site has a directory of members. Information about qualifying to join this organization is provided. Links to other related organizations are included.

Bigfoot
http://www.bigfoot.com
Search tool for e-mail, postal addresses, and telephone numbers.

Board for Certification of Genealogists
http://www.bcgcertification.org/
Web site provides a "Roster of BCG Certified Individuals" and a comprehensive overview of how to become a BCG Certified Genealogist.

Genealib: Librarians Serving Genealogists
http://www.cas.usf.edu/lis/genealib/
Web site and discussion list for librarians who work with genealogical researchers.

Genealogy Helplist
http://www.helplist.org
Volunteers willing to help with look-ups in genealogical records to which they have access.

Genealogy Resources on the Internet
http://www.rootsweb.com/~jfuller/gen_mail.html
List of discussion lists, etc. for genealogical researchers.

Genealogy Software Springboard
http://www.gensoftsb.com/
Searchable database of genealogical freeware, shareware, and commercial prod-

ucts. Software is screened for viruses and other problems and also described and rated. Has a good tutorial on GEDCOM files.

GenConnect Global Surname Search
http://genconnect.rootsweb.com
Search tool for the entire collection of RootsWeb hosted discussions.

GenSeeker
http://seeker.rootsweb.com/search.html
Search tool for Web sites and surnames registered with RootsWeb.

EastEuropeGenWeb
http://www.rootsweb.com/~easeurgw/

HungaryGenWeb
http://www.rootsweb.com/~wghungar/

Internet Address Finder
http://www.iaf.net
Search tool for e-mail, postal addresses, and telephone numbers.

Journal of Online Genealogy
http://www.onlinegenealogy.com/

Random Acts of Genealogical Kindness
http://raogk.rootsweb.com/
Volunteers willing to help with look-ups in genealogical records to which they have access.

ROOTS-L Home Page (Mailing List)
http://www.rootsweb.com/roots-l/

RootsWeb Listing of Genealogical Societies
http://www.rootsweb.com/~websites/gensoc.html

Slovak Republic Genealogy
http://www.rootsweb.com/~svkwgw/

Yahoo!'s People Finder
http://www.people.yahoo.com
Search tool for e-mail, postal addresses, and telephone numbers.

WhoWhere?
http://www.whowhere.com
Search tool for e-mail, postal addresses, and telephone numbers.

WorldConnect
http://worldconnect.rootsweb.com/
RootsWeb family history Web page hosting service and networking tools.

Part 3. Genealogical and Historical Research Organizations

Federation of Genealogical Societies
http://www.fgs.org/

International Internet Genealogical Society (IIGS)
http://www.iigs.org/

National Genealogical Society
http://www.ngsgenealogy.org/

Ohio Historical Society
http://www.ohiohistory.org/
Outstanding example of what a state historical society can provide through its Web site. Growing collection of digitized historical documents, newspaper archives, and the Death Certificates Index for Ohio.

Society Hall Web site
http://www.familyhistory.com/societyhall/

Western Reserve Historical Society Library Web site
http://www.wrhs.org/

Part 3. Libraries, Archives, Cemeteries, Churches, Courthouses, etc.

(See also Cyndi's List categories for these types of sites http://www.cyndislist.com)
(See also The Vital Records search site http://www.vitalrec.com/)
(See also NARA Genealogy page http://www.nara.gov/genealogy)
(See also Ancestry.com Images Online http://www.ancestry.com)

Allen County Public Library (ACPL)
http://www.acpl.lib.in.us/genealogy/genealogy.html

Recognized by researchers as one of the best genealogical collections in the United States. Their genealogical collection rivals larger national libraries. The scope is multi-ethnic and international.

American Memory Project
http://memory.loc.gov
The Library of Congress's growing collection of digitized photographs, movies, sound recordings, as well as historical printed materials that relate to the history and cultures of the United States.

"Archives and Knowledge Management Scholarly Online Resource Evidence and Records for Use by Genealogists and Family Historians"
http://www.dcn.davis.ca.us/~vctinney/archives.htm

Beliefnet
http://www.beliefnet.org
Directory of contact information for thousands of churches, temples, mosques, and other religious/spiritual organizations.

Cemetery Junction Directory
http://daddezio.com/cemetery/index.html

Civil War Soldiers and Sailors System
http://www.itd.nps.gov/cwss/index.html
Searchable databases of military records, battlefields, and national cemeteries for both the Union and Confederate forces in the U.S. Civil War.

Connecticut State Library Web site
http://www.cslib.org/handg.htm
Information about hours and services, catalog of materials, as well as links to the Connecticut historical and genealogical societies' Web sites.

Ellis Island National Monument and Statue of Liberty National Monument Web site
http://www.nps.gov/elis/

Illinois Roll of Honor Search and the Illinois Civil War Veterans Database Search
http://www.cyberdriveillinois.com/departments/archives/databases.html

Illinois State-wide Marriage Index 1763-1900
http://www.cyberdriveillinois.com/departments/archives/databases.html

Index to marriage records for many counties in Illinois during the period 1763-1900.

Library of Congress Web site
http://www.loc.gov/
The source of online materials, information, and access to their catalogs.

Library of Congress, Local History and Genealogy Reading Room Web site
http://www.loc.gov/rr/genealogy/

Making of America Project
http://moa.umdl.umich.edu. (University of Michigan)
http://library5.library.cornell.edu/moa/ (Cornell University)
Collections of searchable page images for more than 6,600 books and 50,000 journal articles scanned from historical books, journals, and other documents.

The NAIL (National Archives Information Locator)
http://www.nara.gov/nara/nail.html
NARA search tool can be used to identify which NARA regional depositories or division of the main NARA location hold a given microfilm title.

NARA Immigration Records overview
http://www.nara.gov/genealogy/immigration/immigrat.html

National Cemetery System Web site
http://www.va.gov/cemetery/index.htm

National Library of Canada
http://www.nlc-bnc.ca/
The National Library of Canada's catalog is searchable online and digital libraries of historical documents, recordings, and photographs are available through their Web site.

National Park Service Web site
http://www.nps.gov
Links to and describes National Park Service managed museums and monuments and libraries and archives available at those locations.

National Society Daughters of the American Revolution Library
http://dar.library.net

National Union Catalog of Manuscript Collections
http://www.loc.gov/coll/nucmc/

Newberry Library
http://www.newberry.org
Web site has search guides for genealogical research that is supported by the Newberry's collection. The scope is multi-ethnic and international.

New York Public Libraries's The Irma and Paul Milstein Division of United States History, Local History, and Genealogy
http://www.nypl.org/research/chss/lhg/genea.html

Repositories of Primary Sources
http://www.uidaho.edu/special-collections/Other.Repositories.html
Maintained by Terry Abraham (tabraham@uidaho.edu) of the University of Idaho Library Special Collections.

State Historical Society of Wisconsin Library Web site
http://www.shsw.wisc.edu/genealogy/index.htmlanswers

UNESCO (United Nations Education, Scientific and Cultural Organization) Archives Portal
http://www.unesco.org/webworld/portal_archives/

Wisconsin State Library Directory of State Library Web sites

http://www.dpi.state.wi.us/dpi/dlcl/pld/statelib.

Part 3. Travel Planning

Travelocity.com
http://www.travelocity.com/
Complete travel services available—car, plane, hotel, specials. Favorite travel site of many librarians.

The Trip.com
http://www.thetrip.com/
Central air travel, car rental, and hotel/motel reservations designed for business travelers. Compares prices, too

Yahoo! Travel
http://travel.yahoo.com/
Central air travel, car rental, hotel/motel reservations, even cruises. Information available for all types of travelers.

Part 3. Adoptee/Birth Parent Information Sites

National Adoption Information Clearinghouse (NAIC) Web site
http://www.calib.com/naic/
The place for all adoptees and birth parents to start researching.

Tina's Adoption Site Web site
http://www.geocities.com/capitolhill/9606/
Provides a compilation of international resources for adoption research including links to legal information and vital records access. This site is compiled and reviewed by Tina M. Musso (tmusso@usa.net).

Part 4. International Genealogical Reference Sites

(See also American Family Immigration History Center
http://www.ellisislandrecords.org/)
(See also Cyndi's List http://www.cyndislist.com)
(See also FamilySearch.org http://www.familysearch.org)
(See also NARA Genealogy page http://www.nara.gov/genealogy)
(See also RootsWeb http://www.rootsweb.org)
(See also all of the sites listed in Parts 2 and 3)

Babel Fish
http://world.altavista.com/
Machine translation of several paragraphs at once from English to Spanish, French, German, Italian, Portuguese, Japanese, Korean, Chinese, or from these langues into English. Babel Fish will also translate Russian to English.

Everton's Genealogical Helper: Web Site International Genealogy Resources page
http://everton.com/reference/world-resource.php

FreeBMD
http://freebmd.rootsweb.com/
Volunteer transcribers publishing birth, marriage, and death certificates on the Web for England and Wales.

FreeReg (UK)
http://freereg.rootsweb.com
Volunteer transcribers publishing baptism, marriage, and burial records from UK sources on the Web.

Immigrant Ships Transcriber's Guild
http://istg.rootsweb.com/

Volunteer project to transcribe and publish ship's passenger lists for researching immigrant ancestors.

Immigration and Naturalization Service Web site
http://www.ins.usdoj.gov
Provides a History, Genealogy, and Education page.

Mexican Border Crossing Records
http://www.nara.gov/genealogy/immigration/mexican.html
Overview on the NARA Web site.

Mexico WorldGenWeb site
http://www.rootsweb.com/~mexwgw/

Morton Grove, Illinois Public Library's Webrary Collection
http://www.webrary.org/ref/genealogy.html
Has selected and annotated the best sites for European genealogical research.

Radix Hungarian Genealogy site
http://www.bogardi.com/gen/

Travlang.com
http://www.travlang.com/
Online translating dictionaries for a variety of languages.

WorldGenWeb
http://worldgenweb.org/
Coordinated site for volunteer GenWeb projects around the world. (See also individual country GenWeb sites cited in previous parts)

World History Archives
http://www.hartford-hwp.com/archives/
Collection of documents for use in teaching World History.

Zacatecas (Mexico) Genealogy page
http://www.geocities.com/Athens/Acropolis/7016/zacatecas/

Part 4. African American Genealogical Reference Sites

(See also American Family Immigration History Center http://www.ellisislandrecords.org/)
(See also Cyndi's List http://www.cyndislist.com)

(See also FamilySearch.org http://www.familysearch.org)
(See also NARA Genealogy page http://www.nara.gov/genealogy)
(See also RootsWeb http://www.rootsweb.org)
(See also all of the sites listed in Parts 2 and 3)

Afrigeneas: African Ancestored Genealogy
http://www.afrigeneas.com/

American Memory Project Collection "Born in Slavery: Slave Narratives from the Federal Writers' Project, 1936-1938"
http://memory.loc.gov/ammem/snhtml/snhome.html

"American Slave Narratives: An Online Anthology"
http://xroads.virginia.edu/~hyper/wpa/wpahome.html

Christine's Genealogy Web site
http://www.ccharity.com/
Home base for African-American Genealogical Research.

"Database of Servitude and Emancipation Records (1722-1863)":
http://www.cyberdriveillinois.com/departments/archives/servant.html
(The Illinois State Archives)

FreedMan's Bureau Online
http://freedmensbureau.com
Records relating to the freed slaves after the Emancipation Proclamation and the U.S. Civil War.

Georgia Historical Society
http://www.georgiahistory.com/

North Carolina State Library
http://statelibrary.dcr.state.nc.us/iss/gr/NCSource.htm

Our BlackHeritage.com
http://www.ourblackheritage.com/

"Slavery and Religion in America: A Time Line 1440-1866":
http://www.ipl.org/ref/timeline/
Published by Carrie Bickner (1998) on the Internet Public Library Web site
http://www.ipl.org

Part 4. Native American Genealogical Reference Sites

(See also American Family Immigration History Center http://www. ellisislandrecords.org/)
(See also Cyndi's List http://www.cyndislist.com)
(See also FamilySearch.org http://www.familysearch.org)
(See also NARA Genealogy page http://www.nara.gov/genealogy)
(See also RootsWeb http://www.rootsweb.org)
(See also all of the sites listed in Parts 2 and 3)

Heard Museum
http://www.heard.org/education/resource/htl.html
Native American history timeline.

Native American Documents Project
http://www.csusm.edu/nadp/nadp.htm

Native American Indian Genealogy Webring Homepage
http://members.tripod.com/~kjunkutie/natvrng.htm

Native American Navigator Project
http://www.ilt.columbia.edu/k12/naha/nanav.html
Historical background needed for productive Native American genealogy research.

NativeNet Web site
http://cs.fdl.cc.mn.us/natnet/
Resources related to Native American history, culture, and current events.

NativeWeb site
http://www.nativeweb.org/
Central location for "Resources for Indigenous Cultures around the World."

Part 4. Heraldry (Coats of Arms, etc.) and Lineage Societies

(See also Ancestor Detective Genealogical Web Site Watchdog http://www.ancestordetective.com/watchdog.htm)
(See also Cyndi's List http://www.cyndislist.com)
(See also RootsWeb http://www.rootsweb.org)

American College of Heraldry Web site

http://members.aol.com/ballywoodn/acheraldry.html
American coat of arms registry and research site.

Associated Daughters of Early American Witches

http://www.adeaw.org/
Lineage society for the descendants of individuals burned as witches in early U.S. history

College of Arms

http://www.college-of-arms.gov.uk
The official office of arms for the United Kingdom.

D'Addezio Genealogy Web site

http://www.daddezio.com/genealogy/articles/registry.html
Article listing offices of arms contact information around the world.

National Society Daughters of the American Revolution (DAR)

http://www.dar.org/
Lineage society for "Any woman is eligible for membership who is no less than eighteen years of age and can prove lineal, blood line descent from an ancestor who aided in achieving American independence. She must provide documentation for each statement of birth, marriage, and death" (Daughters of the American Revolution, 2001).

United Empire Loyalists' Association of Canada

http://www.npiec.on.ca/~uela/uela1.htm
Lineage society for the descendants of residents of the thirteen colonies who remained loyal to the British during the American Revolutionary War.

All Parts. Miscellaneous

50 States.com

http://www.50states.com/

Dictionary.com

http://www.dictionary.com/

The Family Chronicle's Top 10 Genealogical Web sites

http://www.familychronicle.com/webpicks.htm

Family Tree Magazine selects 101 "voted best"

http://www.familytreemagazine.com/101sites/

Genealogy in Fiction
http://ourworld.compuserve.com/homepages/JulieKidd/fiction.htm

"Glossary of Genealogical Terms and Abbreviations"
http://www.genealogy.com/Glossary/glossary.html

Hungary and World War I and II History
http://newmedia.cgu.edu/petropoulos/arrow/history/worldwar.html

"Hungarian Names 101" by Walraven van Nijmegen
http://www.geocities.com/Athens/1336/magyarnames101.html

LizardTech
http://www.lizardtech.com
Publisher of the MrSid image viewing software used by Ancestry.com.

Social Security Administration Publications Page
http://www.ssa.gov/pubs/

The Soundex Machine on the National Archives and Records Administration Web site
http://www.nara.gov/genealogy/soundex/soundex.html

USGenweb site for Pennsylvania
http://www.pa-roots.com/~pagenweb/

More Readings About Genealogical Research on the Internet

The American Heritage® Dictionary of the English Language, Third Edition 1996, 1992. New York: Houghton Mifflin Company. Available online: www.dictionary.com/.

Burroughs, T. 2001. *Black Roots: A Beginners Guide to Tracing the African American Family Tree.* New York: Simon and Schuster.
  The genealogical research strategies discussed in this book are pertinent for any area of genealogical research. The guidance for African American genealogical research is very clear and valuable.

Hinchliff, H. 1994. "Caveat Emptor: The Crest Quest." *National Genealogical Society Newsletter* 20 (6) November/December: 122 and 124.

Hinchliff, H. 1999. "A Right to Bear Arms? An Examination of Commercial Offerings for Henderson of St. Laurence, Scotland." *National Genealogical Society Quarterly* 87 March: 6-9.
  These two articles by the chair of the National Genealogical Society's Ethics Committee discuss some of the historical realities of "family coats of arms," and attempts to profit from individuals' pride in their own surname.

Howells, C. (n.d.) "Researching Your Roots Using the Internet: Cyndi Howells says that the Internet may not be what you think." *Family Chronicle.* Archives available online: www.familychronicle.com/internet.html.
  Excellent overview of the realities of researching genealogy using the Internet and other research formats as well.

Howells, C. 1999. *Cyndi's List: A Comprehensive List of 40,000 Genealogy Sites on the Internet.* Baltimore, Md.: Genealogical Publishing Co. Available online: www.cyndislist.com.
  This is another annotated webliography of genealogical sources on the Internet. It is a printed version of the author's Web site "CyndisList." CyndisList is the most comprehensive genealogical metasite or directory of genealogical Web sites available on the Internet. It is currently sponsored by the RootsWeb organization. This author also wrote the 1997 book *Netting Your Ancestors: Genealogical Research on the Internet.*

Katz, W. 2001. *Introduction to Reference Work, Vol 1.* New York: McGraw-Hill.
  This is the classic introduction to the reference interview, research process, and to the core reference tools that every reference desk staff person needs to know about.

Kavasch, E. B. 1996. *A Student's Guide to Native American Genealogy*. Phoenix, Ariz.: Oryx Press.
Focused on Native American Genealogy, this is also a fine introductory genealogy research guide.

Kemp, T. J. 2000. *The Genealogist's Virtual Library: Full-Text Books on the World Wide Web*. Wilmington, Del.: Scholarly Resources, Inc. (contains CD-ROM; no companion Web site).
This book is an annotated bibliography of full-text sources of genealogical information on the Web. There is no narrative as such beyond the annotations.

Librarian's Genealogy Desk Reference. 2000. Boston: NEHGS (New England Historical Society). Available online: www.genoutreach.org/
This booklet is a recommendation for a core collection of print, CD-ROM, and Internet genealogical resources for libraries. It was distributed at the 2000 American Libraries Association Meeting in Chicago, Illinois. This is highly recommended.

Morgan, G.G. 2001. "Bogus Genealogies." *Ancestry Daily News* January 19. Available online: www.ancestry.com/library/news/articles/3224.asp.

Neill, M.J. 2001. "It's on 1,000 Web Sites." *Ancestry Daily News January 17*. Available online: www.ancestry.com/library/news/articles/3202.asp.

Oxford Encyclopedia of World History.1998. Oxford: Oxford University Press.

Powell-Crowe, E. 2000. *Genealogy Online*, Millennium Edition. New York: McGraw-Hill.
Two full chapters discuss the requirements for getting connected to the Internet and reviews of genealogical database software before we even get to the genealogical research process. Part 2 (chapters 4-8) is primarily a basic Internet tutorial that is very nice—that uses Genealogical research tools as examples to illustrate FTP, Usenet, Mailing Lists, etc. Part 3 (chapters 9-14) is all on specific Web sites, libraries or commercial services. For example, Chapter 9 is Rootsweb, Chapter 10 is on "Online Library Card Catalogs," Chapter 13 is the AOL Genealogical Forum.

Previte-Orton, C.W. 1978. *The Shorter Cambridge Medieval History*. Cambridge: Cambridge University Press.

Reintjes. A. 1990. *How to Research a Little Bit of Indian*. Kansas City, Mo.: American Family Records Assocation.

Renick, B. and Wilson, R. S. 1999. *The Internet for Genealogists: A Beginner's Guide*, Fourth Edition. La Habra, Calif.: Compuology.
This book is written by two experienced genealogical researchers. Significant text is spent on "basic Internet" and the target audience is end-users who are new to the Internet rather than new to genealogical research. The greater part of the book is an annotated webliography of genealogical Web sites.

Stephens-Lamb, T. 2000. *SAMS Teach Yourself Today e-Genealogy*. Indianapolis: SAMS.
Nicely focused on a few selected sites that provide concrete information. The book looks and reads like a demonstration of genealogical Web sites.

Stratton, E. A. 1988. *Applied Genealogy.* Salt Lake City, Utah: Ancestry Inc.
Excellent description of the reasons people choose to do genealogical research, the importance of knowledge of social history and geography, and the need for documentation and verification of genealogical research conclusions.

Sturdevant, K. S. 2000. *Bringing Your Family History to Life Through Social History.* Cincinnati, Ohio: Betterway Books.
Discussion with sources, methods, and case studies for doing family history research.

Swan, J. 1998. *The Librarian's Guide to Genealogical Research.* Fort Atkinson, Wis.: Highsmith Press.
This was one of the first books to integrate Internet resources for genealogical research within a book intended to give librarians general assistance with genealogical research.

Wilson, R. S. 1999. *Publishing Your Family History on the Internet,* Fourth Edition. La Habra, Calif.: Compuology.
This is a companion book to the *The Internet for Genealogists: A Beginner's Guide.* Everything you need to know about Gedcom (genealogical data files) to HTML conversion with descriptions and tutorials of some popular conversion programs. The author also provides basic information about creating a basic Web site, publishing your Web pages on your Web site, and listing your Web site with the genealogical metasites.

Witcher, C.B. 2000. *African American Genealogy: A Bibliography and Guide to Sources.* Fort Wayne, Ind.: Round Tower Books.

Selected Fiction In Which Real Genealogical Research Plays a Role (see http://ourworld.compuserve.com/homepages/JulieKidd/fiction.htm for additional mystery titles)

Adams, D. 1992. *All the Crazy Winters.* New York: Ballantine Books.
The Jesus Creek librarian is murdered and the only thing missing from the library is a copy of a newly published genealogical history of the town. What's in this genealogy that could motivate a murderer? Family pride and family stories are threatened by the reality of genealogical fact.

Brown, R. M. 1994. *Murder at Monticello.* New York: Bantam Books
A century-old murder victim is found buried under the floor of an excavated slave cabin at Monticello. Genealogical research using letters and deeds uncovers the probable story of the murder. Meanwhile the incident sets off a modern murderer whose motivation is also genealogical.

George, A. 1997. *Murder Runs in the Family.* New York: Avon Books.
A genealogist is murdered and knowing the difference between high-quality documented genealogical research and the alternative is pivotal in discovering who is the murderer, as well as who is the victim.

Harrington, J. 1995. *The Death of Cousin Rose*. Aurora, Colo.: Write Way Publishing.
Danny O'Flaherty travels to Ireland to learn more about his Irish grandfather. His "cousin" Rose Noonan is murdered before she can tell him something "interesting" about his grandfather. The motive for the murder lies in nineteenth century parish baptismal records, official birth records, and the laws and traditions governing inheritance of land through primogeniture. Also, beware of digging too deep into your family history—you may discover something that breaks your heart.

Landrum, G. 1992. *The Famous DAR Murder Mystery*. New York: St. Martin's Press
Members of the DAR locating and recording the location of a revolutionary war soldier's grave find a modern corpse. In this story the DAR ladies solve the mystery by doing genealogical research to identify the victim's family and thereby the motivation for the murderer.

Pratchett. T. 1996. *Feet of Clay*. New York: Harper Collins.
Commander Vimes of the Watch solves a series of bizarre murders. The nobility with the assistance of Dragon King of Arms, Head of the College of Heralds, creates a "genealogical" proof that Corporal Nobby Nobs is really the Right Honorable the Earl of Ankh—the bastard scion of the rightful King of Ankh-Morpork. The genealogical proof is based on his name and a medallion left him by his father (who probably stole it from the rightful owner). Head of the College of Heralds, the Dragon King of Arms refuses to give Commander Vimes his family Coat-of-arms as it was recalled/removed when Commander Vimes's ancestor executed the last King of Ankh-Morpork. Never mind that the last king was a complete monster and the entire city had risen up in rebellion against him. But the butcher, the baker, and the candlestick maker are all able to place orders for their own original coats of arms created just for them.

Stratton. E. 1989. *Killing Cousins*. Salt Lake City, Utah: Ancestry Publishing.
Genealogist Mort Sinclair is called in as a police consultant to assist in investigating a series of murders on a small island where everyone is related in some way. The motive for the murders is genetic. Mort must clarify the real family relationships to identify the patterns of who has been killed, to predict who will be next, and finally to identify which member of this small genetic pool is the murderer.

Tolkien, J.R.R. 1965. *The Return of the King* (Part III of the Lord of the Rings, Second Edition). New York: Houghton-Mifflin Co.
The family trees of the Baggins, Cottin, Tooks, and Brandybucks families, as well as the lineages of the Kings and Stewards of the Numenorean lines are part of the appendices beginning on p. 313.

A Concise Glossary of Genealogy and Internet Terms

For definitions of additional genealogy terms see Genealogy.com's "Glossary of Genealogical Terms and Abbreviations" (available online: www.genealogy.com/Glossary/glossary.html).

Ancestor
A relative from whom you are descended. For example parents, grandparents, great-grandparents, etc. Ancestors are usually someone with whom you share a genetic connection or a connection by social or legal agreement at some point in your lineage.

Ancestral File
Genealogical data format system and database used by the LDS Church. The Ancestral file format is a standard format for genealogical data. The Ancestral File database publishes international genealogical data for millions of individual ancestors and families.

Ancestry
See also Direct line, Family tree, and Lineage.
The documented line of individuals going back in time with which you are related genetically.

Birth records
Documents that record the birth of an individual. Official birth records usually provide the mother's full maiden name and the father's full name, the name of the baby, the date of the birth, and the county and municipality where the birth took place. Family and church birth records and historical official records may contain more or less information. Birth record information will vary depending on who the recorder (healthcare professional, parent, etc.) was and when and where the recording was made.

Cemetery records
Cemeteries sometimes maintain records of names, death dates, and locations of burials. Some cemeteries also keep records of the names and addresses of relatives. Gravestones also contain information, such as the birth and death dates of the deceased person and sometimes names of family members such as parents and spouses.

Census records

Censuses are basically a count of the population or a political unit such as a country, state, city, county, etc. Many censuses collect additional demographic information, such as names, ages, occupations, addresses, citizenship status, and ethnic background. The first U.S. Federal Census was in 1790. The Constitution of the U.S. requires a national census every ten years for the purpose of clarifying congressional representation for each state. Individual states and cities have also conducted censuses. Most other countries also conduct censuses regularly and historically.

Church records

Formal documents that many churches and other religious organizations keep. Church records record christenings, baptisms, marriages, burials and other ceremonies and religious events. These records can be valuable for confirming the name(s) of the individuals involved, the date and location of the event, and thereby the location of a particular time. Sometimes information about witnesses to an event including parents' names, godparents'/sponsors' names, and their location at a particular time.

Death records

Record of the death of an individual. Generally death records provide the name of the individual, the date, and the location of the death. Some death records provide names, addresses, occupations, and ethnicity of the deceased and sometimes witnesses to the death or family members. The name and address of an attending physician is frequently provided on more modern death records.

Descendant

The genetic or legal offspring of an individual, e.g., children, grandchildren, great-grandchildren.

Direct line

See also Lineage.
Genealogical phrase describing a one-to-one connection between persons directly related to each other, e.g., parent and child.

Discussion lists

Discussion lists are formal Internet communications tools used by people to discuss as a group topics in which a group is interested. Discussion lists may operate by using e-mail—mailing lists—or by using threaded discussion software on or through a Web page—Newsgroups or E-forums. When someone sends a message to a discussion list, everyone who belongs to or is subscribed to that discussion receives a copy of the message.

Download/downloading

This is the process of copying files from another computer to your computer. On the Web this is usually accomplished by "saving" a file located on the Web to a local computer hard drive.

E-journal/e-newsletter

A journal, magazine, or newsletter distributed in electronic form.

E-mail

Electronic mail. Messages, notes, or letters sent between people through computer accounts.

Family

Social group of individuals related genetically or by social agreement. All of an individual's ancestors taken as a group.

Family group sheet

Format used by the LDS church which presents genealogical information about a nuclear family—a husband, a wife, and their children. A family group sheet has spaces for birth dates and places, death dates and places, and marriage dates and places.

Family histories and genealogies

These may be informal as when a genealogist compiles unpublished documentation of a family history and genealogy or this phrase may refer to books or articles that publish genealogical information about a particular family or group of families. Family history and genealogy books and articles are only as reliable as the documentation they are based on.

Family tree

See also Ancestry, Direct line, and Lineage.
Genealogical diagram of a family's ancestry. The totality of an individual's ancestors and descendants.

Freedman

Person released from slavery or emancipated. This term is used to refer to both male and female individuals.

GEDCOM

An acronym for GEnealogy Data COMmunications, GEDCOM is a standard format for genealogy databases. The standard format simplifies the exchange of data between different database programs.

Genealogy

See also Family tree and Lineage.

Research and documentation of the descent of a person, family, or group from an ancestor or ancestors; a family tree.

Internet

The international network of computers. In order to be on the Internet a computer must have Internet connection software (dial-up, cable, etc.) and have an Internet Service Provider or be on a network connected through an Internet Service Provider.

Lineage

See also Ancestry, Direct line, and Family tree.

Documented and traced descent from a particular ancestor or group of ancestors.

Logon/login

Procedure to identify yourself to a computer system or database as an authorized user. Normally, to login you need to type in a valid user name and password. The word "login" is also used.

Logout

Disconnecting from a computer system or database. The word "logoff" is also used.

Maiden name

The surname a woman is born with. Sometimes the term birth name is used. In the past in many European countries and in the U.S., it was common practice for a woman to take her husband's surname on marriage or for her to be referred to as "wife of" in legal or religious records (e.g., in medieval Magyar records: "a woman's official name is constructed from her husband's name by adding the suffix -ne to his given name. As an example, a woman named Anna who is married to Tar Jakab (bald Jacob) would be recorded in official documents and would introduce herself in polite company as Tar Jakabne (bald Jacob's wife). This is similar to the English practice of using Mrs." (Hungarian Names 101, 1998).

In modern times many women choose not to use their husband's surname on marriage.

Mailing lists

See Discussion lists.

Marriage records

Record of a formal, religious, or legal marriage between two individuals. Generally marriage records provide the name of the individuals, the date, and the location of the marriage ceremony. Some marriage records provide names, addresses, occupations, and ethnicity of the marrying couple, as well as their parents and the witnesses to the marriage.

Maternal line

See also Family tree and Lineage.
Genealogy traced through the maternal ancestors, e.g., mothers, grandmothers, great-grandmothers, etc.

Metasite

Web site that collects, organizes, and frequently reviews other Web sites. Most metasites are organized by subject.

Naturalization records

Documentation of immigration from one country to another and the process of becoming a citizen in the new country. Official naturalization records document place and date of birth, date of arrival into the new country, places of residence during the process of naturalization. Some historical naturalization records provide the name of the ship and the port of entry. Others contain information about occupation and physical descriptions of individuals.

Netiquette

Basic etiquette for communicating with other people through the Internet. Use the same good etiquette used in in-person communication. Courtesy and respect for others' time and privacy are paramount.

Newgroups

See Discussion lists.

'Plug-in' software

Software that a Web browser uses to reproduce sound, graphics, and video on your computer, e.g., Real Player.

Primary source

Records that were made by a witness or witnesses to an event or by an official agent based on witness testimony, contemporarily or at about the same time as a life or historical event. Official birth, death, marriage, or other legal records are usually primary sources. Bible and other family records may also be primary sources.

Secondary source

Records or compilations of records, articles, books, etc. based on primary sources. Some records, especially vital records, may be primary sources of one kind of information but secondary sources of another. Marriage and death records are primary sources for the marriage and death dates but secondary sources for birth dates. Articles, books, and other compilations of information are only as reliable as the documented primary sources they are based on. Interviews (oral histories) with living or contemporary individuals are secondary and sometimes tertiary sources.

Soundex

Surname index based on the way a name sounds.

Surname

Last name; family name.

Tertiary source

Compilations of records, articles, books, etc based on secondary sources.

URL (The Universal or Uniform Resource Locator)

International standard address format used to designate a Web site or other Internet service on the Web.

Vital records

See also Birth records, Marriage records, Death records.
Vital records are official or family documents of vital or life-affecting events.

Web browser

Software installed on a computer that is then used to access Web pages and other Internet services. Netscape Communicator and Internet Explorer are examples of World Wide Web browsers.

Web page

Individual publication on the Web that may contain text, software, graphics, or multi-media.

Web site

Internet computer location designated by a URL, where Web pages or other Internet service is located.

World Wide Web (Web)

An Internet-based service that publishes text, graphics, software, and multi-media through Web pages that make up Web sites. An Internet connection and Web browser software such as Netscape Communicator and Internet Explorer are required for access to materials published on the Web.

Index

S

T

U

V

W

About the Author

Diane K. Kovacs founded Kovacs Consulting — Internet & Web Training in 1993, while employed as a reference librarian at Kent State University. In 1995, she started training and consulting full-time. Her training experience has been entirely with adults, mainly with library or research services staff members. Mrs. Kovacs's primary training area has been Internet subject research, including genealogical research. She first formally taught "Genealogical Research on the Internet" in 1996.

Mrs. Kovacs enjoyed working with many genealogy researchers as a reference librarian. She began researching her own family because she found talking about her family history with her parents, grandparents, and many great-uncles and great-aunts to be a rewarding and interesting activity. She has been interested to find that her ancestors originated from many different parts of Europe including Germany, France, and England and has found one Civil War veteran, and is working on documenting a Revolutionary War ancestor. She and her father-in-law work together to trace her husband's family's roots in Hungary. She occasionally assists other family members to research ancestors from Mexico (Zacateca), Spain, and North Africa.

She received an M.S. in Library and Information Science from the University of Illinois in 1989 and an M.Ed. in Instructional Technology from Kent State University in 1993. A vitae is attached and also online at www.kovacs. com/dianevitae.html.

Mrs. Kovacs has written several other books that are both training manuals and guides for trainers. Most of the books have a companion Web site that enhances the contents of the printed book. Some of her published work includes:

How to Find Medical Information on the Internet: A Print and Online Tutorial for the Health Care Professional and Consumer co-authored with Ann Carlson (Berkeley: Library Solutions, 2000).

Building Electronic Library Collections: The Essential Guide to Selection Criteria and Core Subject Collections (New York: Neal-Schuman, 2000).

The Cybrarian's Guide to Developing Successful Internet Programs and Services (New York: Neal-Schuman, 1997).

The Internet Trainer's Total Solution Guide (New York: Van Nostrand Reinhold/John Wiley, 1997).

The Internet Trainer's Guide (New York: Van Nostrand Reinhold/John Wiley, 1995).